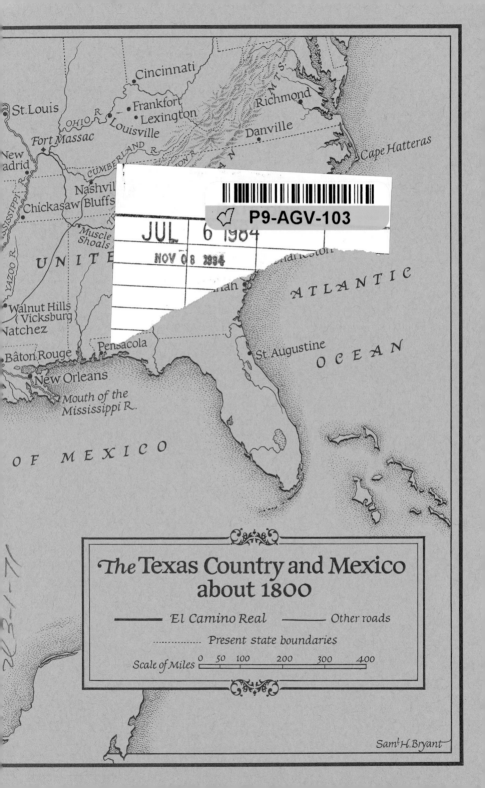

St. Louis

OHIO R.

Fort Massac

CUMBERLAND R.

New
Madrid

MISSISSIPPI R.

YAZOO R.

Walnut Hills
(Vicksburg)

Natchez

Bâton Rouge

New Orleans

Mouth of the
Mississippi R.

OF MEXICO

Cincinnati

Frankfort
Lexington
Louisville

Nashvil

Chickasaw Bluffs

Muscle
Shoals

UNITE

Richmond

Danville

Cape Hatteras

ATLANTIC

OCEAN

Pensacola

St. Augustine

JUL 6 1984

NOV 08 1994

P9-AGV-103

The Texas Country and Mexico
about 1800

——— El Camino Real   ——— Other roads

.... Present state boundaries

Scale of Miles   0   50   100   200   300   400

Saml H. Bryant

MEN WITHOUT COUNTRIES

Books by
JOHN EDWARD WEEMS

Men Without Countries

Peary: The Explorer and the Man

Race for the Pole

The Fate of the *Maine*

A Weekend in September

❧ ❧

M E N
WITHOUT COUNTRIES

Three Adventurers
of the Early Southwest

BY

JOHN EDWARD WEEMS

ILLUSTRATED BY RICK DUIKER

BOSTON

HOUGHTON MIFFLIN COMPANY

1969

First Printing   R

Copyright © 1969 by John Edward Weems
All rights reserved. No part of this work may be
reproduced or transmitted in any form by any means,
electronic or mechanical, including photocopying and record-
ing, or by any information storage or retrieval system,
without permission in writing from the publisher.

Library of Congress Catalog Card Number: 69–19567
Printed in the United States of America

FOR

Donald, Carol, Mary, Barbara, Janet,
and their great-grandmother,
Mrs. W. E. Weems

❧ ☙

Breathes there the man, with soul so dead,
   Who never to himself hath said,
      This is my own, my native land!
Whose heart hath ne'er within him burn'd,
As home his footsteps he hath turn'd
      From wandering on a foreign strand?
If such there breathe, go, mark him well . . .

> — *The Lay of the Last Minstrel,*
> SIR WALTER SCOTT

Youngster . . . if you are ever tempted to say
a word or to do a thing that shall put a bar
between you and your family, your home and
your country, pray God in His mercy to take
you that instant home to His own heaven.

> — *Philip Nolan in "The Man Without
> a Country,"* EDWARD EVERETT HALE

ACKNOWLEDGMENTS

BENNETT LAY of Houston, biographer of Ellis Bean, suggested Philip Nolan to me as the subject of a book. After initial research into Nolan's fascinating life, I decided to add to it appropriate periods from the careers of Nolan's intriguing associates, Wilkinson and Bean.

My wife, Jane, gathered virtually all of the primary-source material used in this book. Commencing in 1961, during visits to archives, she acquired a more intimate knowledge of three roguish men and wild horses than any woman ought to have.

A number of librarians have been especially helpful: Dorman Winfrey, who was archivist of The University of Texas Library when research began for this book and who is now Texas State Librarian; Chester Kielman and his staff of The University of Texas Archives Collection; Llerena Friend and her staff of the Barker Texas History Center; and the staff of the main library of The University of Texas.

My thanks also to John Banta of Waco, Texas, and James B. Irwin of Blum, Texas, for taking time to talk with me about Philip Nolan.

In 1961 four other librarians provided assistance. Their names and positions at that time: Elenora Gralow, librarian, Fisk Public Library, Natchez, Mississippi; David C. Mearns, chief, Manuscript Division, Library of Congress, Washington, D.C.; John E. Regard, director, Louisiana State Archives and Records Commission, Baton Rouge; and Ruth K. Robbins, acting librarian, New Orleans Public Library.

CONTENTS

CONTENTS

MEN WITHOUT COUNTRIES

1. THREE OF A KIND

JAMES WILKINSON, Philip Nolan, and Peter Ellis Bean all were born in the tumultuous eighteenth century. Although they came from divergent backgrounds and seemed destined for three vastly different courses in life, each man was to be bound eventually to a common self-interest: an acquirement of the riches, real or imagined, to be found westward beyond the Mississippi River. This was then, however, territory belonging to His Catholic Majesty, the King of Spain, whose suspicions of such fortune-seekers pressing in from the east were making hunting increasingly hazardous for them.

Each man was to exhibit, also, certain common characteristics, although in varying degrees: a general willingness to sacrifice loyalties to family, friends, and country whenever the pliability would enhance Opportunity, and an ability to call forth exceptional intensities of charm and deviousness for the same purpose. "All these men have their price," the British statesman Sir Robert Walpole had said of some eighteenth-century contemporaries. The quotation also could have been applied to Wilkinson, Nolan, or Bean, born in that same century, and to a great many of their contemporaries.

Wilkinson, born in 1757 amid the billowy Maryland hills, was fourteen years older than Nolan, whose birthplace was the teeming Irish seaport of Belfast. Bean, much the youngest and the least sophisticated of the three, was a true son of the frontier, born in 1783 to a family whose members, male and female, were quick to fight. His birthplace was on the dark Holston River in what was to be Grainger County, Tennessee.

Nolan was a common denominator linking the three men; Wilkinson and Bean possibly never met, certainly not until a time late in both their lives. When a youth Nolan became the protégé of Wilkinson, probably while Wilkinson was engaged in commerce and politics in Kentucky, and in any event before Wilkinson became ranking general of the United States Army. Bean later was to sign on as a member of one of Nolan's filibustering expeditions into Texas — the last one, it proved to be.

All three men shared a common fate. Each one died far from his native land, unmourned for long except by one or two or three individuals, and in generally unhappy circumstances, which were largely the result of a lifelong division of loyalties. Of the three, however, only Wilkinson seems to have been chronic in his duplicity. Nolan and Bean apparently were educated into it — Nolan as a protégé of the preying Wilkinson, and Bean by necessity, as will be seen.

Wilkinson is the most widely known of the three, because of his role in the Revolutionary War and his later activities in the trans-Allegheny region of the young United States. Bean is virtually unknown, except to a reader with an abiding interest in Texas history. Nolan is largely misknown, because of a slip made by Edward Everett Hale in a short story published during the Civil War. Hale's story, still familiar to many Americans, was entitled "The Man Without a Country," and his central character was a man named Philip Nolan.

Hale had read James Wilkinson's *Memoirs of My Own Times* some time earlier and had noticed Wilkinson's numerous references to his protégé. Later, when he wrote "The Man Without a Country," Hale chose the name Nolan for his central character. Remembering incorrectly — he believed the first name of Wilkinson's protégé and trusted assistant to have been Stephen — he used "Philip" in his story. Through this accident of fiction Philip Nolan has become mostly a mythical character; but though Hale's story and Nolan's actual biography have virtually nothing in common, "The Man Without a Country" does have some coincidental pertinence to Nolan and to his associates, Wilkinson and Bean.

Hale, who was a much-respected Unitarian minister of Boston as well as a prodigious author, wrote his story for a purpose: to inspire patriotism at a critical period in United States history. The nation was locked in its Civil War, and Union fortunes had waned early. Dissatisfaction at several levels had infiltrated the North, and in New York City a series of draft and racial riots in 1863 killed some two thousand citizens. Further division threatened.

In the story, the fictional Philip Nolan was portrayed as a United States Army lieutenant who had come under the influence of Aaron Burr, the man known in North American history for his alleged plot to carve out a kingdom of his own somewhere to westward. In a noisy trial in Virginia that actually took place, Burr was acquitted of treason, but in a trial that never occurred except in Hale's imagination, Philip Nolan was found guilty of a similar charge. When asked by the president of the military court if he had anything to say in extenuation, Nolan exclaimed, as Hale wrote it, "D—n the United States! I wish I may never hear of the United States again!"

Shocked by Nolan's eruption, the court retired to a private room and, after a fifteen-minute delay, returned to give Nolan his wish: "The Court decides, subject to the approval of the President, that you never hear the name of the United States again."

For the next fifty-five years, from September 23, 1807, until the day he died, May 11, 1863, the fictional Nolan never again heard the name of his country. He was held prisoner on board United States Navy ships, at sea and on foreign station, first on one vessel then another, for the rest of his life, and never was allowed to return to his native land. Written material given to him was scanned first, and any references to the United States were scissored out.

"No mess liked to have him permanently," Hale wrote, "because his presence cut off all talk of home or of the prospect of return, of politics or letters, of peace or of war, — cut off more than half the talk men like to have at sea."

Nevertheless, the fictional Nolan was liked personally, and he was treated courteously by officers and men. He soon came to hunger for word from home — silently, for he never allowed himself to voice this yearning until his last day. In time "he loved his country as no other man has loved her," as he indicated once, while speaking to a midshipman attached to his prison vessel.

Youngster, let that show you what it is to be without a family, without a home, and without a country. And if you are ever tempted to say a word or to do a thing that shall put a bar between you and your family, your home, and your country, pray God in His mercy to take you that instant home to His own heaven.

Amid the dissent common to the last half of the twentieth century, such advice, particularly quoted out of context as it is here, will only be scoffed at by many Americans, but Hale's narrative, in its time, was an effective contribution "towards the formation of a sentiment of love for the nation." Even today "The Man Without a Country" is recognized as a classic and as an example of the best of Hale's writing, much of which was mediocre.

When the story appeared it seemed so realistic that many readers accepted it as an authentic account. Hale mixed fancy with fact in such a way that an entirely unlikely tale became an apparently true story, and though he was careful to declare it an invention, many Americans continued to grieve over the plight of Philip Nolan and to wonder at the events that snared him as a shipboard prisoner for more than half a century.

The New Orleans *Daily Picayune* of May 15, 1864, printed the comment of a man who knew better. In a letter to the editor signed "D. de Goicouria," the man wrote, "The *Atlantic Monthly*, of December last, has published a curious story, entitled 'The Man Without a Country,' which has been extensively copied by the newspapers of this Republic and of Europe." He continued:

> ... The author has given dates, names of officials and vessels of war and intends this ingenious story to be taken as a literal fact. But as Phillip [sic] Nolan really existed and his name is connected with the early history of Texas, I feel much pleasure in giving you a brief sketch of his life, which I have derived from a collection of historical documents now in possession of J. A. [Quintero], Esq., who obtained them of the Mexican authorities from the Spanish archives at Monterey. . . .
>
> Phillip Nolan was a handsome and a brave man. He, like an Indian, felt at home in the desert and in the forest. He was, however, an accomplished scholar, endowed with fine talents and rare scientific and literary attainments. He made the first map of Texas, which he presented to the Baron of Carondelet, then Governor of Louisiana. His journals contain valuable information in reference to the resources and geography of Texas; also on the refractions of heavenly bodies in altitude, which he observed during the year 1800, and an account of the different Indian tribes which inhabited that country, its medicinal plants, etc. . . .

De Goicouria's sketch of Nolan's life, not entirely quoted above, was itself distorted and exaggerated — at least insofar as can be determined now, because the documents once in the possession of Quintero have apparently vanished. Nevertheless, this Nolan obviously was not the Philip Nolan of Edward Everett Hale's story, and when Hale became aware of the slip — on his own initiative, in rereading Wilkinson's Memoirs — he determined to rectify what he presumed to have been an injustice to the real Nolan.

Hale traveled to Louisiana and Texas to gather material for

a biography of the man. After some investigation he commented:

> The part which the real Philip Nolan played in our history is far more important than that of many a man who has statues raised in his honor. So far as careful work among memorials of his life would serve, I have tried to rescue him from the complete oblivion which hangs over him. He was murdered by the Spanish Government, who dishonored their own passport for his murder. Were such an event possible now [1877], war within an hour would be the consequence. . . . But Spain was strong then, and America was weak, and Mr. Jefferson was pacific.

Hale used his Nolan material not in a biography — for surely not enough of it existed for such a purpose — but in an inferior novel, *Philip Nolan's Friends*. Ironically, in his fictionalized story he made several major mistakes in recounting the real Philip Nolan's life, so that instead of "rescuing" Nolan, Hale actually contributed further to the mythology enveloping him. Hale made Nolan into a thoroughly admirable, dashing, daring hero, a man of great loyalty and integrity, an American patriot who was cruelly murdered by Spain. Slain he was, but the briefest investigation into contemporary documents will show that Nolan was not the undefiled man Hale portrayed. He was actually even more of a man without a country than Hale thought. Wilkinson and Bean showed similar lapses of loyalty.

In *Philip Nolan's Friends* this statement appears in a eulogy for the dead Nolan:

> Poor fellow! how often I have heard him say that he did not know what country he served, or what army gave him his commission.

Hale thus came near the truth, unintentionally, about Nolan; and the same words could have been used to describe Wilkinson and Bean, but for one exception. Wilkinson and Nolan and Bean knew at all times which country they served, though this might have seemed to vary from time to time.

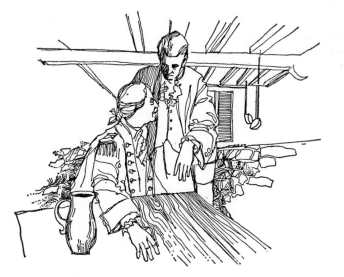

2. LAND OF TOMORROW

WHEN YOUNG JAMES WILKINSON, having completed one
career, prepared to loosen the fruitful soil of Kentucky in
order to sow his hopes for a new fortune, he had already acquired a collection of experiences worthy of a man twice his
age.

He was the second son of a respected merchant-planter
whose comfortable residence near Benedict, Maryland, on
Hunting Creek, stood in an area of rich earth, plentiful game,
and deep rivers: the Patuxent, Severn, Potomac, Susque-
hanna. After James's birth, in 1757, two sisters had arrived.
This family, however, was short-lived: when James was about
seven his father died. The only paternal admonition he was

able to catch and hold at such an early age were Joseph Wilkinson's words that proved to be his departing ones: "My son, if you ever put up with an insult I will disinherit you." Years later, James Wilkinson, in his *Memoirs*, was to remember this sentence clearly, after a lifetime of lashing out at those who affronted his honor.

His father's death probably contributed to James's early maturing. And from his widowed mother (he said in his *Memoirs*) he acquired "a sound constitution, my sense of justice and of the Christian faith." The gentility of his Maryland home imbued him with an appreciation of grace and beauty in life — including attractive, intelligent women. His father's estate provided sufficient financial support to give him a casualness toward money, a trait that stayed with him later, to his misfortune, after his wealth had vanished.

The family income enabled him also to have a competent education. It might have been superior, but James was not a particularly good student. Nevertheless, in 1773, around his seventeenth birthday, his mother sent him to medical school in Philadelphia, where two extracurricular activities also occupied considerable time: making the acquaintance of important Philadelphians, such as the Biddles, and consorting with officers of the 18th Royal Irish Infantry, whose colorful uniforms and precise drills thrilled him greatly, as he stated in a description of his first visit to the army post.

> On approaching the gate . . . I beheld a man under arms, in complete uniform; he was a centinel . . . whose appearance rivetted my attention: after surveying him attentively from head to foot, I passed without obstruction and entered the barrack yard, where the first, and I may say only, object that struck my eyes, was the troops on parade at open order, which exhibited a more impressive spectacle than I had ever seen;

indeed, I was fascinated, and gazed with astonishment at the promptness and uniformity of the manual exercise which they performed; but when the ranks were closed, and the line was wheeled into column, — marched, — recovered its ground, — closed and displayed, I was struck with the idea of a painted wall, broken in pieces and put in motion; it appeared like enchantment, and my bosom throbbed with delight . . . and from that day I felt the strongest inclinations to military life.

When the Irish infantry left Philadelphia in 1774 for Boston, where, after the historic Tea Party, open revolution threatened, Wilkinson did not lose his military zeal.

Nor did he lose it after he had begun medical practice in Monocacy, Maryland, at the age of eighteen. Whereas in Philadelphia he had been admiring a group of Royal Irish, however, in Maryland he volunteered for service in a rifle corps of the revolutionary forces.

Then began Wilkinson's phenomenal rise in the military service. Although he would never excel in field command — his decisions, quickly made and often altered, tended to be based on superficial considerations — he and army life soon became compatible. James Wilkinson won notice as a quick, interested, able young man. He also learned the right thing to say and the right way to say it, which won him further notice, but he disguised his sycophancy well enough. His most efficient Revolutionary War service was as somebody's aide.

In a variety of ways he paid court to those who could advance his career: while on the staff of General Nathanael Greene; and as a nineteen-year-old commander of an infantry company; then as aide to the capable, if later discredited, General Benedict Arnold, during Arnold's expedition to Canada.

Wilkinson became a brigade-major near his twentieth birthday, on July 20, 1776, and a lieutenant colonel some six months later. He served at Trenton, Princeton, and Saratoga; attracted the interest of General George Washington and of General Horatio Gates, among others; was appointed adjutant-general to the Army of the Northern Department of America by Gates on May 24, 1777, and was brevetted brigadier general on November 6 of the same year. Thus he reached his majority and generalship about the same time.

Wilkinson's Revolutionary War service seemed meritorious except for two notable flaws. After General Burgoyne had surrendered at Saratoga, New York, Wilkinson was entrusted by General Gates with a report to Congress discussing the capitulation, and Wilkinson stretched his momentous 285-mile journey from Albany to York, Pennsylvania, where Congress was then meeting, into a trip that took him almost two weeks. At Easton he was detained two days by the charms of a lovely visitor from Philadelphia — Ann Biddle, whom he would marry in 1778 — and at Reading he lay over for another two or three days, in shelter from a series of violent downpours that he feared would aggravate a lingering illness. When he finally arrived at York he learned that the news he bore had already been received and disseminated. Nevertheless, he delivered Gates's report — and, incidentally, a recommendation from the general for Wilkinson's promotion, urged by Gates with the assertion that he had not seen a more promising genius. One congressional critic proposed giving Wilkinson a pair of spurs instead of a promotion, but the advancement, which was the brevet of brigadier general, was nevertheless bestowed on him in the happiness of the occasion.

Wilkinson's stop at Reading had led to the second major indiscretion of his Revolutionary War service. At Reading he had been a dinner guest of William Alexander Stirling, an American general, and in the ebullience produced by drink and an interested audience Wilkinson had spoken intimately to one of Stirling's aides of an intrigue involving his patron of the moment, General Gates, and Thomas Conway. Conway, a soldier of fortune who had held a Continental commission as a general, was plotting to effect the displacement of Washington by Gates. Thus the word of the notorious Conway Cabal leaked out: first to Stirling, who communicated it to Washington himself. Gates's subsequent feeling toward his once-trusted subordinate can be imagined, but Wilkinson sent up a smokescreen of excuses, blame shifts, and a climactic duel challenge to Gates, and he somehow managed to extricate himself with regard to the general, without fighting the duel. The Continental Army was a different matter, however, and Wilkinson was virtually forced out of it — through resignation of assigned duty — until 1779, a year after his marriage into the influential Biddle family, when the army sought to utilize his considerable staff ability as clothier general. Wilkinson's appointment to that post came, however, only after two others had refused to take the job.

About the same time he purchased a 444-acre estate near Philadelphia, named it Trevose, and commenced to devote most of his attention to its management and to an assumption of a major role in Philadelphia society — to the exasperation of long-enduring General Washington, who began pressing Wilkinson to shape up. With the clothier general's interest in military clothing flagging anyway, from a level that never was high, Wilkinson again resigned in March 1781.

His new family, Trevose, and politics then occupied his attention, but though his family flourished, Trevose did not. His wife, Ann, who had transgressed her Quaker faith by marrying a general, bore him a son in 1781. Eventually there were to be four children, but the last one died when very young. Meanwhile, Trevose and Wilkinson's financial situation both languished, and even some success in politics — election to the Pennsylvania Assembly from Bucks County — failed to satisfy him. At the age of twenty-six he needed a new country, one equal to his ever-expanding ambition, and he began looking westward across the Appalachian Mountains to Kentucky, a territory named from an Indian word that some said meant "land of tomorrow" and others said meant "dark and bloody ground."

Whatever it meant, land was to be had there, and land had become the great American commodity; the young nation possessed or produced little else of much value, certainly nothing in such great quantity. With English Canada lying to the north and Spanish Florida to the south, the spillover toward free and open country could only flow westward. There, men like Wilkinson reasoned, land could only increase in value as immigrants flocked into the new republic to enjoy the freedom it guaranteed, and as the population otherwise soared.

In choosing Kentucky James Wilkinson selected a luxuriant region, but one bubbling in ferment. There was the constant threat of Indians, and the settlers there, cut off by the mountains from the rest of the United States, comprised a very individualistic population. Nevertheless, the land held hope and promise, prospects that especially appealed to Wilkinson now, and descriptions of it proved to be powerfully attractive — like this glowing, but overstated, report which appeared in a book published in the early nineteeth century, *Sketches of History, Life and Manners in the West:*

> Every thing here assumes a dignity and splendour I have never seen in any other part of the world. You ascend a considerable distance from the shore of the Ohio [River], and when you would suppose you had arrived at the summit of a mountain, you find yourself upon an extensive level. Here an eternal verdure reigns, and the brilliant sun of lat. 39 piercing through the azure heavens, produces, in this prolific soil, an early maturity, which is truly astonishing. Flowers, full and perfect as if they had been cultivated by the hand of a florist, with all their captivating odours, and with all the variegated charms which colour and nature can produce, here, in the lap of eloquence and beauty, decorate the smiling groves. Soft zephyrs gently breathe on sweets and the inhaled air gives a voluptuous glow of health and vigour, that seems to ravish the intoxicated senses. The sweet songsters of the forest appear to feel the influence of this genial clime, and, in more soft and modulating tones, warble their tender notes in unison with love and nature. Every thing here gives delight; and, in that mild effulgence which beams around us, we feel a glow of gratitude for the elevation which our all bountiful Creator has bestowed upon us. . . .
>
> From Limestone to Licking Creek, the country is immensely rich, and covered with cane, rye, and the native clover. . . . [Cane] is an evergreen, and is, perhaps, the most nourishing food for cattle upon earth. No other milk or butter has such flavour and richness as that which is produced from cows which feed upon cane. Horses which feed upon it work nearly as well as if they were fed upon corn, provided care is taken to give them, once in three or four days, a handful of salt. . . .
>
> The buffalo are mostly driven out of Kentucky. Some are still found on the head waters of Licking creek, Great Sandy, and the head waters of Green river. Deer abound in the ex-

tensive forests; but the elk confines itself mostly to the hilly and uninhabited places.

The rapidity of the settlement has driven the wild turkey quite out of the middle counties; but they are found in large flocks in all our extensive woods.

Amidst the mountains and broken country are great numbers of . . . grouse . . . and since the settlement has been established, the quail, following the trail of the grain which is necessarily scattered through the wilderness, has migrated from the old settlements on the other side of the mountain, and has become a constant resident with us. This bird was unknown here on the first peopling of the country.

Well enough for the scenery and the gentler natural life, but what about the dangers of living in this wilderness? The author of the preceding sketch neglected to mention some of the hazards, failed to describe a panther's demoniac howl at midnight, which sometimes sounded like "the wail of a child in agony," or the appalling war whoop of an Indian, both heard much too frequently in isolated cabins miles from the nearest neighbor. Even after the Indian threat had been effectively contained in Kentucky, roving bands of savages occasionally swept down from north and west of the Ohio River to plunder and kill.

Early Kentucky history bristled with tales of these Indian depredations, like the one involving a noted frontiersman and Indian fighter, Simon Kenton, and a few companions who once followed a band of marauding savages northwestward across the Ohio with the aim of retrieving some stolen horses. In *Sketches of History, Life and Manners in the West*, published while Kenton was still living, appeared an account of his ordeal, which, if exaggerated, nevertheless illustrated the cruelties of which the Indians were capable.

After several days of following the culprits, the Kentuckians arrived in the vicinity of the Indian village, where they hid until after dark. Then, well into the night, they crept toward the village as only experienced backwoodsmen could have done, recovered the stolen horses, took some of the other mounts, and fled toward Kentucky.

The Indians overtook Kenton on the bank of the broad Ohio River and captured him there. Promising him a ride on one of their best horses, they forced him astride a vicious young animal, bound him securely to avoid a fall, and released the mount. Kenton's horse reared, bucked, and plunged through the thick woods in its frenzy to dislodge the rider, who was sometimes banged against tree limbs and other times shredded by dense thickets. Eventually, the horse wearied of its unsuccessful effort and fell in quietly behind the Indian party returning to the village, even pausing occasionally to graze.

Kenton's respites were brief, however, for whenever the Indians had moved on out of sight the horse would seem to panic in its solitude and race after the vanished warriors, carrying the victim's lacerated body through the brush and scraping him against overhanging branches.

At the village Kenton was removed from his horse, smeared with a black tar, and tied to a stake. There he remained for hours, contemplating a slow death from his torturers. Instead, he was released at the end of that time and forced to run a gauntlet through two rows of Indians of both sexes and all ages. They whipped him with switches and sticks until he was nearly dead.

He survived, however, and later managed to escape. He eventually returned to Kentucky, then moved to Ohio, where he died years later near the site of his torture.

No one was exempt from these dangers, and mere existence

demanded intelligence and determination. Another tale told of how a party of Indians crept through the shadowy Kentucky forest toward a solitary log house, sent one man ahead to reconnoiter, and waited. The savage saw that only a white woman, a Negro man, and two or three children occupied the cabin at that moment, and he rushed inside without waiting for assistance. He seized the Negro just as the woman grabbed an ax, the nearest weapon, and with a quick blow felled the Indian, who lay on the floor, motionless, in a spreading puddle of blood. The children, instead of freezing in terror, slammed the door and fastened it before the remaining Indians had advanced to try to force their way in. Then the quick woman again turned the attack. She seized a stockless gun barrel nearby, pointed it at the savages through an opening between the logs, and frightened them into fleeing.

To the frontiersmen who preceded Wilkinson the land had been worth these trials. Even before settlers began flocking into Kentucky during the Revolution and in the years immediately following, King George III had not been able to keep men out. In a 1763 proclamation he forbade white settlement west of the Appalachian Mountains, preferring to keep his colonists where he could observe them — near the seacoast, which was within easy reach of England's naval power. Nevertheless, men like Daniel Boone, John Finley, and James Harrod were not deterred: despite King George's edict they came to Kentucky to look it over, and in Harrod's case to survey it, for future residence.

As the written accounts indicated, they found a region forested with magnificent stands of pines, oaks, sycamores, chestnuts, and walnuts; watered by clear rivers and pure springs; enriched in its central — or bluegrass — region by especially fertile soil. The diversified face of the land was sufficient to please many people. From the mountainous eastern and southeastern region, where the soil was not so rich, the country devolved into gently undulating terrain. Along the northern boundary ran the Ohio River; to the west, the Mississippi, where particularly fertile bottomland was to be found.

Into this country the tide of immigration carried Wilkinson and others, not like the swelling billows of the ocean, overwhelming all the land in one vast torrent (commented an early writer), but like the gradual overflowing of a great river: breaking over banks, forming channels, spreading into small pools, and finally inundating the land. Some settlers brought all their possessions by boat down the Ohio River; others crossed the mountains in the spring of the year, leaving families behind to assure that a crop would be raised while they looked over the new land. In the fall they returned for their kin.

Beyond the perils, Wilkinson's chosen land afforded an adequate existence, even to a man who had not the means to live as well as he. A settler with a family need have only an ax, a rifle, and a horse — all three of the best possible quality — then he could provide himself with most of the other necessities.

His home, wood throughout, came entirely from the surrounding forest. Logs formed the walls; plain surfaces of split logs, upturned, provided a smooth floor. The door, composed of split logs, was held together firmly by wooden pins, hung on wooden — or sometimes leather — hinges, and fastened with a wooden latch. If the family was large, other cabins were built as necessary.

The frontiersman used wood also to make his furniture, prepared skins for shoes and other apparel, grew corn, potatoes, squash, and pumpkins, and killed deer, bear, and turkey for his table.

This was the primitive country to which James Wilkinson turned, but such a grandee as he was not coming to fell trees for log cabins. By the time Wilkinson arrived, in fact, the choice section of Kentucky was not really a poor man's frontier: speculators, who had been attracted early, already were demanding high prices for some acreage, especially in the bluegrass section.

Still, the American tide flowed in, always in search of something better. This was a national trait that had been aptly discussed earlier by an English colonial governor, Lord Dunmore, in a letter reproduced in *The Conquest of the Old Southwest*, by Archibald Henderson.

The established Authority of any government in America, and the policy of Government at home, are both insufficient to restrain the Americans. . . . They acquire no attachment to Place: But wandering about Seems engrafted in their Nature; and it is a weakness incident to it, that they Should for ever immagine the Lands further off, are Still better than those upon which they are already settled.

3. THE BENEFACTOR

WILKINSON came to Kentucky as a merchant and a land speculator, representing at first Philadelphia business interests. He put Trevose up for sale, left his family behind to care for the property, and departed for the new country in the fall of 1783, when twenty thousand settlers were said to have moved into the territory. By December he had made entries for land tracts located near Lexington and Louisville.

A former general attracted attention on the frontier, and as word spread of Wilkinson's presence, people observed him closely. A contemporary, Humphrey Marshall, saw him this way:

> A person not quite tall enough to be perfectly elegant, compensated by symmetry and appearance of health and

strength; a countenance open, mild, capacious, and beaming with intelligence; a gait firm, manly, and facile; manners bland, accommodating and popular; and address easy, polite and gracious, invited approach, gave access, assured attention, cordiality and ease. By these fair terms, he conciliated; by these he captivated.

Wilkinson impressed even the socially elite with his air of refinement; yet he mixed with all people easily and won the friendship of the multitudes. He gained this approval largely through facile oratory on popular subjects, delivered in a musical voice and permeated with florid language appropriate to the eighteenth century, and through sumptuous entertaining.

All of his traits combined to produce a favorable first impression, but many persons found that their initial enchantment lost ground in future dealings. To many of his perceptive fellow citizens, Wilkinson was much too gregarious, pretentious, and pompous, and he was absolutely without humor, although some persons were to regard him as a funny man. A contemporary called his style "turgid." His singular rise in military rank and his other successes at such an early age had multiplied his egotism; and even at twenty-six his self-indulgence had become evident in the fleshiness emphasized by his stubby frame. His profile, described by some who knew him as handsome, was said to lose impact when Wilkinson appeared head-on, and an observer saw a face too broad and too round, one reflecting his inherent haughtiness.

Nothing, however, could detract from Wilkinson's special strength. For his time and place he was sly — not brilliant, not endowed with great depth, for he frequently underestimated a person's comprehension of Wilkinsonian pretense —

but he was shrewd enough in fast dealings, and he impressed undiscriminating frontiersmen with his smattering of knowledge in many areas: medicine, military affairs, law, business, education, politics. He was quick to acquaint himself with a peculiar situation, by which he hoped to benefit, regarding trans-Appalachian river transportation, the only type feasible as a commercial outlet for the eighteenth-century Western Country.

The Mississippi River was the key to the transportation system. It drained more than one-third of the present United States, and its combined waterways open to commercial use exceeded a total of fifteen thousand miles, although their extent was not fully realized then. These western rivers were, in Wilkinson's day, the only means of commercial transport for goods in quantity.

In years past this western area had belonged to France. In 1762, however, that nation had ceded to Spain its holdings west of the Mississippi River — and the "Isle of Orleans," on which stood the city of New Orleans — shortly before she would have been forced to surrender them to Great Britain at the end of a lost war. Early the very next year, England did indeed take other French holdings, including Canada and territory east of the Mississippi, in a settlement agreed upon at Paris.

These French lands had never been self-supporting, as had the English colonies on the Atlantic Seaboard, and Spain agreed, somewhat reluctantly, to assume control of New Orleans and the western region, primarily because possession would provide a buffer between the English colonies — and their probable expansion — and the Spaniards' own cherished domain of Mexico.

During the American Revolution, Spain and France supported the independence movement, not because of affection
for the revolutionists, but because of hatred and fear of their
old enemy, Britain. During the war the Continental Army
had been able to procure powder and other supplies from
New Orleans, transporting the goods, with much difficulty,
up the western rivers.

Then, in the 1783 Treaty of Paris, which recognized American independence, the agreement between Great Britain on
one side and France, Spain, and the United States on the
other, stipulated that navigation of the Mississippi River to
the sea was to be open to commerce of the United States as
well as to that of the other three nations.

Spain quickly became fearful of the potential of her new
neighbor to the north, however, and was not at all desirous of
encouraging further growth by allowing Americans unlimited
access to what could be a rich trade outlet. Soon after the independence had been won, Spain began using her control of
New Orleans and the mouth of the Mississippi to constrict
trade, despite the 1783 agreement, and in 1784 closed the
river to American use.

Still, the westerners found shipments might get through, or
might not, depending on the momentary attitudes and moods
of Spanish officials. One of their victims was a man named
Thomas Amis, who arrived in Natchez in June of 1786 with
a cargo of flour and iron castings, bound for New Orleans and
transshipment from there. The Spaniards confiscated his
goods and sent him home, where he publicized his grievances
and further inflamed his fellow citizens.

Even when the Spaniards allowed Americans to sell their
merchandise it was usually at an arbitrary price that always

favored the Spaniards. Still, the profits could be great, even if the gamble was large. Western men continued to try to beat the capricious Spaniards, who were certainly not frightened out of their hostile actions by any armed might of the United States, because little might was then in existence. The new republic had been organized under a loose Articles of Confederation, in which the central government — if it could be dignified by calling it that — was empowered only to recommend measures to the thirteen states, all of which seemed to spend their time tugging at each other.

Further weaknesses were evident, especially in regard to Kentucky. The region was legally a part of Virginia, but mountains separated the parent state from its dependent. Travel back and forth was slow; a one-way trip might require three weeks. Because of this remoteness, the Virginia government felt little inclined to spend money on Kentucky, even for defense against the Indians, yet Kentucky was not allowed to act for itself in many matters.

Dissatisfaction over being ignored soon developed in the West, and this feeling, combined with the frontiersman's inherent desire for complete freedom of movement, motivated some people to voice a desire for independence not only from Virginia, but from the new republic as well. Such talk coming later in United States history would have been clearly treasonable, but it was not considered necessarily so at this time, at least not by everyone, because the nation was not far removed from one revolution that had separated it from established government.

One western area did, in fact, proclaim its independence from the United States, then openly courted the Spaniards — the "State of Franklin," in what is now East Tennessee. One

of its leaders, John Sevier, wrote the Spanish minister in Philadelphia in 1788 that the people of Franklin "infer that their
interest and prosperity depend entirely upon the protection
and liberality of your government."

Explanation of the laxity of attitude peculiar to that day
is provided by four written extracts:

Edward Everett Hale's elaboration on his fictional Philip
Nolan, who had damned his country, mentioned several actual
reasons for loyalty being split in the trans-Appalachian region:

> [Nolan], on his part, had grown up in the West of those
> days. . . . He had been educated on a plantation where the
> finest company was a Spanish officer or a French merchant
> from Orleans. His education, such as it was, had been per-
> fected in commercial expeditions to Vera Cruz, and I think
> he told me his father once hired an Englishman to be a
> private tutor for a winter on the plantation. He had spent
> half his youth with an older brother, hunting horses in Texas:
> and, in a word, to him "United States" was scarcely a reality.

In a 1780 letter to Governor Edmund Randolph, a prominent Kentucky politician, Harry Innes, openly discussed separation.

> . . . I am decidedly of opinion that this western country will,
> in a few years, Revolt from the Union, and endeavor to erect
> an Independent Government; for under the present system,
> we can not exert our strength, neither does Congress seem
> disposed to protect us, for we are informed that those very
> troops which Congress directed the several states to raise for
> the defense of the western country are disbanded. I have just
> dropped this hint to your Excellency for reflection; if some
> step is not taken for protection, a little time will prove the
> truth of the opinion.

Another prominent Kentuckian, Thomas Green, raised the

possibility of separation in a 1786 letter to the governor of Georgia, but in this case with the cooperation of the British, who had agents in the Western Country working toward that end. "Great Britain," said Green, "stands ready with open arms to receive and support us."

Even Thomas Jefferson, when elected President near the end of the eighteenth century, was to admit the possibility of separation. "If they [the West] see their interest in separation," he wondered, "why should we take sides with our Atlantic rather than our Mississippi descendants? It is but the elder and younger brothers differing. God bless both and keep them in the Union, if it be for their good, but separate them, if it be for the better."

This attitude was not shared by everyone, but many residents of the Western Country felt no inspiration to hold firmly to any ideals, and the region lay ready to be led to a new destiny. James Wilkinson observed, listened, mused over the possibilities, then acted. He would lead the people west of the Appalachians out of their plight. In doing this he would replace an earlier spokesman, George Rogers Clark.

In Kentucky Wilkinson at first peddled salt, bolts of cloth, liquor, saws, and other frontier goods — in addition to speculating in land — and he traveled frequently. In 1784 his wife and family joined him in Lexington, where he opened a store — which he soon neglected for real estate and politics — and built a mansion. Two years later he moved to the present site of Frankfort, where he erected a tobacco warehouse on a tract of land he had purchased, and built another mansion. He laid out the town of Frankfort, which was to become the Kentucky capital.

Wilkinson also occupied himself with a series of assemblies, beginning in 1784 at Danville, in which Kentucky delegates discussed problems of their region: statehood, or possibly another form of independence; free access to the Mississippi; Indian defense. Sometimes Wilkinson was a delegate, sometimes not. Whatever his capacity, and whether or not he was present, he offered verbose advice — and people listened. He strongly supported autonomy for Kentucky and unlimited use of the Mississippi; and together with all other western men he was inflamed by recurring rumors that Congress planned to abandon United States claims to passage down the river in exchange for certain Spanish trade considerations that would accommodate Eastern Seaboard states. In a letter written in 1786 he declared, "Congress, by not asserting the right of the Union to the navigation of the Mississippi, a right derived from Nature and founded on Treaty, betray the trust in them."

The rumors out of the capital at Philadelphia were not without substantiation. John Jay was pressing for a treaty with Spain in which the United States would abandon any claim to the Mississippi for twenty-five years, and George Washington tended to agree with him. These two men, and others, apparently did not foresee the rapid growth of the West and the vital role of the river.

Washington, however, early realized the mood of the westerners. In a 1785 letter he had written, "The emigration to the waters of [the Mississippi] are astonishingly great and chiefly of that description of people who are not very susceptible to law and order and good government. It will be difficult to restrain people of this class from enjoying natural advantages."

Another time he wrote Colonel Henry Lee, then a congressional delegate, "It may require some management to quiet the restless and impetuous spirits of Kentucky, of whose conduct I am more apprehensive in this business than I am of all the opposition that will be given by the Spaniards."

Again he wrote Lee, one month later, "There are many ambitious and turbulent spirits among [Kentucky] inhabitants, who, from the present difficulties in their intercourse with the Atlantic States, have turned their eyes to New Orleans, and may become riotous and ungovernable, if the hope of traffic with it is cut off by treaty."

Amid these rumors of abandonment of the West, Wilkinson won election as a delegate from Fayette County to the Third Assembly in August 1786. There a proposal championed by him to give Kentucky statehood was introduced and promptly passed. Wilkinson became a delegate also to the Fourth Assembly a few months later, and in a letter he boasted:

> I carried my Election 240 ahead & find by the observations of several Bystanders, that I spoke 3½ Hours, instead of 1½ as I think I before mentioned. . . . I pleased myself, &, what was more consequential, every Body else, except my dead opponents — these I with great facility turned into subjects of ridicule and derision. I have experienced a great change since I held a seat in the Pennsylvania Assembly. I find myself . . . much more easy, prompt, & eloquent in a public debate, than I ever was in private conversation, under the greatest flow of spirits.

Wilkinson's fellow citizens again elected him a delegate to the Fifth Assembly in September 1787, but this time he did not attend. Apparently impatient with the nonproductivity of assemblies, he had loaded a cargo of tobacco, bacon, and flour, and with typical cocksureness had gone directly down-river to New Orleans, to talk with the Spanish governor, Esteban Miró. Wilkinson's charm, his former title as United States general, and his clever use of gifts at hostile Spanish military posts along the way enabled him to reach the forbidden city, where Miró actually received him soon after his arrival on July 2, 1787.

Wilkinson found Miró to be a generous, somewhat complacent administrator who resembled himself in some ways — particularly in his endeavors to supplement official salary, which never seemed adequate for his sumptuous entertaining. He also found a man worried about the "Anglo-American threat" to the Spanish domain, as were a great many of Miró's associates. From a peak in 1621, when the Spanish empire was known as the greatest in world history, Spain gradually had been weakened by poor administration and corruption so that, by Miró's day, its strength had waned badly, and wise Spaniards recognized this.

What Wilkinson and Miró talked about was not known — not at that time, anyway — but Wilkinson was allowed to sell his cargo, and he stayed in New Orleans until the middle of September, when he returned by ship to the United States. He arrived at Wilmington early in November, then traveled to Richmond, where he became involved in the latest political haggle: the question of adopting a new, and stronger, federal Constitution. Wilkinson spoke out against it — apparently, some presumed, because he reasoned that the rumored surrender of the Mississippi claim would follow its adoption. He returned home to Lexington in numbing February weather, but he warmed quickly in the company of lovely Ann Biddle

Wilkinson, who was her husband's most consistent admirer and who gave up her attachments in the East to accompany him to the Western Country and its vicissitudes, its loneliness.

Soon after his return a bustle of activity developed, centered around the Wilkinson mansion. Wilkinson sent a messenger to Danville with a letter to Harry Innes. The messenger returned the next day with Innes himself, who joined Wilkinson in a private discussion on topics of which only they were cognizant. Soon after that, the same messenger departed, with two companions, in a canoe bound for New Orleans.

Most of Wilkinson's fellow Kentuckians who heard rumors of these mysterious occurrences presumed that they concerned his business dealings. Nor were they suspicious when they heard talk of letters being carried to New Orleans by the messenger: Wilkinson had negotiated an agreement with Spain for the use of the Mississippi, and his popularity had never been higher. Because of the new trade outlet, Kentucky tobacco could bring $9.50 a hundredweight instead of $2.00, flour $7.00 and more a barrel instead of $2.50. As another result, food prices in western Pennsylvania rose sixty percent by early 1790. Wilkinson anticipated that much of this profit, of course, would go to himself: he would buy at Kentucky prices and ship the goods to New Orleans. The increased trade activity would nevertheless help to promote the entire region, not just one man, and James Wilkinson could rightly consider himself its benefactor.

4. A DEVOTED SON

WILKINSON'S varied commercial activities demanded the assistance of a trustworthy, capable man who could subordinate himself completely to Wilkinson's massive egocentricity. In past transactions — and in future ones, so it was to prove — Wilkinson failed to command for long the loyalty of his business associates, largely because of his outsized self-esteem. He and a partner in his first Lexington venture — the store — soon split in mutual indignation.

Wilkinson chose Philip Nolan, and Nolan proved to be absolutely loyal to his patron. When or where Wilkinson found him is not clear — perhaps when Nolan was a boy in Maryland, where he was believed to have lived for a time.

Wherever it was, Wilkinson could not have engaged a more effective man for his service.

Nolan was endowed with a large share of Irish acumen, and he was strong, courageous, energetic, and persuasive. He also was a young man with a surprising degree of polish for the frontier; this quality proved to be especially impressive to persons of importance, both American and Spanish.

Nolan has been described, not surprisingly, as "dashing and handsome" by some writers, and the reports of his romances with quick-eyed ladies would seem to substantiate this. Probably, however, he was more dashing than handsome. Edward Everett Hale once saw a now-vanished portrait of Nolan: "a miniature of him elegantly set in gold, which represents rather a bluff face, apparently Irish, of a man about thirty." Hale thought Nolan's appearance disappointing.

Contemporary descriptions of Nolan help to visualize him. Wilkinson, in his *Memoirs*, wrote of his protégé: "Sanguine, volatile and enthusiastic, his enterprising spirit could not be restrained, by prudential considerations; and in colloquy, or familiar correspondence, the ardour of his imagination, frequently transported him beyond the rules of ordinary expression."

In a letter written to Governor Manuel Gayoso de Lemos of Louisiana May 25, 1790, Wilkinson discussed him further: "[Nolan] has lived two years in my family and I have found him honorable, discreet, courageous and active."

Even the Spaniards later were to join in the acclaim. Another Louisiana governor, Don Francisco Louis Hector, Baron de Carondelet, called Nolan a "charming young man whom I regard very highly," and a "young man of talents, good breeding, and moderation." Governor Manuel Muñoz of

Texas added his praise in a letter in which he mentioned Nolan's "industrious nature . . . natural comprehension . . . [and] knowledge of geography." Nolan's own handwriting — compact, legible, careful, and correct — bespoke a man with a good education, however he acquired it. Sometimes his frequent division of paragraphs gave the impression of a man in a hurry.

Nolan's birthplace was Belfast, Ireland, and the year of his birth 1771, according to information he was to give a Spanish census taker during a sojourn in Nacogdoches, Texas, in 1794. He was also listed at that time as single, but he probably was not then a very lonely bachelor — and no doubt never was.

Other information on Nolan's early life is scarce. Some persons speculate that Wilkinson reared and educated Nolan, basing their belief on certain correspondence: Nolan to Wilkinson, June 10, 1796 — "[you,] the friend and protector of my youth"; Wilkinson to Gayoso, September 22, 1796 — "[Nolan] a child of my own raising"; Wilkinson to Thomas Jefferson, May 22, 1880 — ". . . An acquaintance of many Years, from his Early Youth."

Some of these descriptions, like "a child of my own raising," have a ring of figurative speech. Probably Nolan did not become a member of the Wilkinson household until the late 1780's — in 1787 or 1788, as a letter from Wilkinson of May 25, 1790, to Gayoso would indicate — although the two might have become acquainted earlier.

In his *Memoirs* Wilkinson discussed the matter further: "It is true, this extraordinary character was first my *protégé*, and afterwards my agent, in Louisiana, and that he took charge of my affairs in the years 1789–90 and 91." In another instance Wilkinson said Nolan became his agent in 1790.

Whatever the exact date, these were the years when Wilkinson was using his influence with the Spaniards to keep the Mississippi River trade open for the inhabitants of the Western Country, and Nolan became his most trusted assistant during that period — a fact that was to add considerably to the knowledge of Nolan's character many years after both men were dead.

Not even Wilkinson's personal enemies could dispute the degree of his influence now, and his admirers became ecstatic. Daniel Clark, Jr., an energetic, intelligent New Orleans businessman who was Wilkinson's friend during this period, said of him, "For some time all the trade of the Ohio was carried on in his name, a line from him sufficing to insure to the owner of the boat every privilege and protection he could desire." Kentucky farmers and merchants, with the exception of those Wilkinson had alienated in close personal dealings, thought of him as the savior of the West.

Even more than the West apparently had been saved. Wilkinson's commercial activities bore the appearance of success to those who had known of his earlier financial plight. He offered to buy tobacco and other Kentucky crops at prevailing prices, or even at somewhat higher figures, for transfer downriver to the New Orleans market.

In the spring of 1788 Wilkinson dispatched a large cargo shipment, in charge of a business associate and a friend from Revolutionary days, Major Isaac Dunn, a brooding man who, like Wilkinson, had been a physician. Wilkinson himself did not plan to make the trip.

To help Dunn supervise the voyage of his fleet, Wilkinson

sent Philip Nolan, whose self-assurance belied his age of seventeen years. The two would oversee a cargo of tobacco, flour, and other provisions, much of which had been stored hopelessly in Kentucky warehouses for years.

Nolan's main responsibility probably was to look out for the goods, to prevent pilfering. Considering his inherent curiosity and his devotion to any job, however, he surely studied the river and its navigation thoroughly on these early trips. What he saw was the beginning of a bustling traffic that would reach a peak more than half a century later with the use of steamboats.

No steam was available for propulsion, however, in Nolan's day. Only the current, or sometimes sails, or the toil of men could move a boat from one place to another on rivers of the West. Going downstream presented no problem other than keeping a close watch for navigational hazards, but this required constant care, for the river held many dangers. Submerged trees, or "planters," which had toppled into the stream when the swift current caved in river banks, dropped their heavy root ends to the bottom and lay silently in wait to stave in a boat. Usually they were most dangerous to vessels coming up the river, because the current pointed their trunks and branches downstream, like spikes. Another underwater hazard were "sawyers" — planters whose free ends bobbed up and down with the current.

Still another danger was the mighty current itself, which was so powerful in the Mississippi River that by the late eighteenth century it had changed much of the river's course since La Salle explored it a century earlier. The force of the water racing toward its freedom in the Gulf of Mexico sometimes crumbled banks and swept away islands in a matter of hours, and it was capable of carrying with it into the Gulf two thousand cubic feet of gravel, rock, silt, and good topsoil every second. During a flood, authorities have estimated, the Mississippi could sweep away farming soil at the rate of forty acres a minute.

To navigate these waters, tradesmen like Wilkinson, Dunn, and Nolan relied on a variety of boats. The few vessels built at this time to make two-way voyages — up as well as down-river — offered testimony to the drudgery men would endure to earn their dollar a day and coarse ration. Except when conditions permitted hoisting sails for a struggle against the current, never-ceasing effort by crews was required to inch a vessel upstream — by rowing, warping, poling, or towing by hand. Of the four methods, poling was most commonly used when water depth and the river bottom permitted.

A narrow walkway ran along each side of a boat designed for upriver travel. Crewmen, each equipped with an iron-tipped pole, walked aft down these ways, the tipped end gouging into the river bottom and the other end pressing against a reinforced shoulder pad worn by the poleman. As the men walked aft, the boat crept forward, always at the pace of a slow pedestrian. When each man reached the stern, he raised his pole out of the water, ran forward, and reset it to begin the ordeal again. The work was grinding, and it was especially unpleasant in rain or snow. Whiskey from a nearby barrel fueled the human machines: a cup every hour, usually, washed down by the same amount of murky river water.

Despite all this effort, poling was easier than some other methods used to gain upriver mileage. When the use of poles became unfeasible because of water depth or a soft bottom, the crew used a cordelle, or towline, to haul the boat against the current — and their own sinew provided the sole power. One end of the line, about a thousand feet long, was affixed to the mast and rigged forward in such a way as to prevent swinging the boat; the other end went into the hands of the hapless crewmen who swam or waded ashore with it. Then the work began: tugging furiously, the men hauled their boat upriver despite many obstacles that hindered their progress. If the brush became too thick to work through, they hacked out a passage with axes. If Indians threatened, they carried rifles to defend themselves.

One river story told of still another problem. On the Mississippi between St. Louis and the Ohio towered a hundred-foot cliff, named the Cornice Rocks, which was used by the cordelle men as a walkway in pulling their boats. In warm weather, the men discovered, the snake population nearby enjoyed sunning itself on this cliff. One boat crew found amusement and a degree of satisfaction in kicking some of these snakes over the cliff and upon their keelboat, and the blasphemous captain, far below.

Even a cordelle was not the most arduous way to work upstream. When neither poling nor the cordelle proved feasible, a captain resorted to warping, a method used especially by heavy boats such as barges. Two small boats, one ahead of the other, alternated in carrying lines or cables from the barge to the shore. After the first line had been secured to a tree, the barge used its capstan to pull itself upstream on the line. Meanwhile, the second line would have been on its way to another tree farther up the river, and when it was secured there, the boat would pull itself up another several hundred feet.

River boatmen, before steam, did not sneer at any possibility for propelling themselves upward against the current, however ridiculous the effort might have appeared to an ocean sailor. Sometimes they even used tree limbs: grabbing one, they would walk aft with it to the stern, release it, and hurry forward to grasp another and repeat the process.

Under these conditions respectable progress sometimes measured eight miles a day or less. A trip from New Orleans to Cincinnati might require a hundred days, New Orleans to Pittsburgh four months. A steady walker could have outdistanced most boats struggling upriver, but, slow as they were, they finally arrived with the cargo, with good luck; and no other way of bringing the goods then existed.

Boats most frequently built for round-trip travel on western rivers were long, slender, double-ended keelboats, as much as eighty feet long and eighteen feet wide, capable of carrying from fifteen to thirty tons; and giant barges, usually longer and wider than keelboats, with a capacity of from forty to one hundred tons or even more.

The most commonly used boat when Nolan made his first trip for Wilkinson, however, was the flatboat — or "Kentucky" or "New Orleans" boat, or "broadhorn," so named for the two or more long, oarlike sweeps that extended over both sides to keep the boat well in the current. These boats served only one purpose: loaded, to run with the current to New Orleans. There, in a city that needed good lumber, the captain and crew unloaded goods, then broke up the boat, sold it along with the cargo, and walked home up the eastern bank of the Mississippi; or, less frequently, bought passage in some deep-water vessel bound for a port on the Eastern Seaboard.

Oak or pine trees, left unseasoned to reduce the expense,

went into the construction of these flatboats, which usually ranged in length from twenty to one hundred feet and in width from twelve to twenty feet. Forward, a raked bow allowed an increased speed, however slight, through lower water resistance. Astern, a roofed house afforded protection for cargo and for men. Usually it was furnished with a brick fireplace and chimney — definite assets on damp, chilly days. Occasionally the roof covered the entire boat.

Flatboats proved to be economical. The cost ranged from one dollar to a dollar and a half a foot, making the price of a fifty-foot- long "flat" at around seventy-five dollars. The addition of a pump and a fireplace, considered first-class equipment, added ten dollars apiece, but the length of the trip made the expense worthwhile. Even though all flatboats headed downstream, voyages from Pittsburgh to New Orleans — nearly two thousand miles — still required as long as five or six weeks, and from Louisville to New Orleans — about fourteen hundred miles — one month. Probably one-fourth of the flatboats never reached their destination, historians have estimated, because of sinking, grounding, capture by river pirates, or destruction by Indians. High insurance rates, up to ten percent, or even more, of cargo value, reflected these dangers.

Such was the river situation when Major Dunn and Nolan accompanied Wilkinson's cargo shipment of 1788. In late spring they departed from a point below the tricky falls of the Ohio, a stretch of rapids at Louisville especially dangerous when the river was low. Then, it was said, the roar could be heard far away, and a boat crew needed to be agile, quick, and strong to negotiate the falls safely. Men accomplished it, however, as also they labored upstream against an almost relentless current; but Wilkinson wisely instructed his boatmen to gather downriver from the obstruction.

Little is known of this or any other Wilkinson shipment, except for a few impersonal details regarding costs and profits. Some documents show that in 1789 Wilkinson paid flatboatmen thirty-five dollars for the one-way trip to New Orleans, and that he once paid out for insurance a fee representing one-sixth of the total value of his cargo. Of Nolan's and Dunn's observations and experiences, or those of the men who went with them, nothing is known now; but the trip can perhaps be reconstructed briefly on the basis of contemporary accounts of river travel.

The clumsy flatboats would have been lashed together, two or more in a bunch, for better speed — by presenting a broader combined surface to the current — and for companionship and protection during the long trip. The joviality and excitement of the largely inexperienced crews as they pushed away from the Kentucky shore into the swiftly flowing Ohio River can be imagined; the current would sweep them southwestward toward a junction with the Mississippi, thence southward to distant, fabled, foreign New Orleans. The early-morning chill would give way to warmth as they proceeded southward.

Veteran rivermen would have had fewer illusions about the joys of a trip. On board the barges, the sturdy Creoles hired from Canada or Louisiana might have been cheerful enough, but Creoles were rarely unhappy, even while engaged in exhausting river work. On the keelboats, the lean, loud American boatmen who comprised most of the crews might have cast vague thoughts toward the joys available down the river, but as river veterans they would have realized that much day-by-day toil separated them from these pleasures. The work would be broken only by rough, contrived diversions like fighting and wrestling, or by spontaneous battling with townspeople along the way, or by more peaceable amusements like singing, storytelling, or listening to the fiddler, a character of singular importance on the river, like a cook on the cattle range. Always the most immediate escape, however, was the whiskey barrel, and almost every boat had one.

Some veteran rivermen surely would have been in Wilkinson's fleet, but a great many of the crewmen no doubt were farmers and knockabouts. Possibly this was Nolan's first trip to New Orleans, and considering his affinity for demanding work and his confidence in mastering each situation as it arose, his exhilaration at floating free with the current must have been great.

A large shipment required care, however, and the voyage grew long and tedious, even though the river had begun its rise with the spring flood and the current flowed more swiftly. By day the men kept watch for planters, sawyers, and other submerged snags, and for eddies. Aft, atop the house, a steersman strove to keep the boat clear of danger and steady in the stream by guiding the vessel with a long oar that reached into the water from atop the roof. Especially treacherous were bends of the river, where the current played tricks, and upstream points of islands, where driftwood and other debris frequently formed a tangled barrier past which the current rushed hazardously. Guiding an awkward flatboat around these obstructions required skill, patience, and strength.

Most unpleasant physically, however, were the occasional groundings, which sometimes caused the cheaply built boats to disintegrate, with a resultant loss of cargo, and frequently resulted in an immersion for all occupants. When a "flat" ran aground, everyone was obliged to leap over the side to help push it clear. No one was excepted — not even a paying passenger, if one happened to be aboard. Two consolations could soothe the waterlogged victims afterwards: survival and a drink from the whiskey barrel.

Wilkinson's men probably did not attempt night navigation; few crews did. Any river by night was too hazardous. Before dark most boats "headed to," and their wearied occupants stretched their legs ashore. After supper, which was cooked and devoured quickly, without much regard for taste, came a few hours of relaxation: stories, usually bawdy; gambling, often heated; songs, frequently rollicking and sometimes resembling sea chanteys.

Swarms of mosquitoes added their high hum to the music, but the men became inured to this annoyance, too, and the frolic continued late after so long a day. Finally, after the last song had been sung, the last oath rasped, and the last sexual encounter painstakingly described, they spread their blankets and slept until dawn, when the hard world began turning for them again.

Southward down the Mississippi the weather changed. Often the mornings rolled in with a thick fog that delayed departure; midday became uncomfortably warm and humid. The appearance along the banks changed somewhat, too. Long moss, or "Spanish beard," hung from giant trees, cutting off sunlight further and creating an atmosphere of gloom. Compensating for this discomfort was the growing nearness of Natchez, which even then had begun to acquire a little of its later notoriety as a site of rivermen's debaucheries.

The town came to offer a double excuse for carousing. To

boatmen bound down the river for New Orleans, it meant the end of what many of them considered the most hazardous part of the journey, and the first chance for a spree. To those bound up the river, and to the men walking home from New Orleans, it stood as a last-chance place of pleasure. To protect the genteel inhabitants from such vulgarity, in Spanish days boatmen were not allowed atop the hill, where the elite lived, without a permit from the commandant.

South of Natchez the river swept Nolan and his companions along the last two hundred miles or so to New Orleans. On arrival there, June 15, 1788, they found a low-lying city, protected by a constantly expanding dike begun years earlier. The city was divided into French, Spanish, and American communities, with the French predominant: it was French by birth and French in soul, and the French inhabitants rarely condescended to mingle with other residents except in matters of business. New Orleans was, however, temporarily out of character at this time.

Three months earlier the city had been ravaged by a fire that destroyed nearly a thousand buildings, and many of the five thousand inhabitants were in the throes of rebuilding. Furthermore, Governor Miró had instituted certain austerities upon the commencement of his term in 1786. By his order, stores were to remain closed during hours of divine service, women were not "to pay excessive attention" to dress, taverns were not to cater to soldiers, Negroes, or Indians, and gambling was outlawed. Spanish military patrols, thoroughly detested by the French populace, enforced these and other laws, but the soldiers were hamstrung: the Spanish authorities ordered them to use weapons sparingly to avoid further antagonization of the French, and they were instructed to follow this practice even when, as frequently happened, a French crowd besieged them to free a fellow Frenchman who had been arrested for some infraction.

Neither the fire nor Spanish arbitrariness could stifle for long the Frenchman's yen for fun: dancing, racing, the carnival, and the theater. Furthermore, neither prevented Wilkinson's cargo from being sold. The General's share of the money later was deposited with a local firm, Clark & Reese. By July he had received more than nine thousand dollars, but out of this came Dunn's share — more than three thousand dollars — and payments of another three thousand dollars or more in bills. Still, prospects appeared bright, and the Spanish officials appeared to be very sympathetic to Wilkinson.

Governor Miró himself seemed most cooperative of all. When Daniel Clark, Sr., Wilkinson, and Dunn formed a company to develop Kentucky–New Orleans trade, Miró suggested that the firm stock a boat to carry cargo up the river all the way to Kentucky. Philip Nolan, still in New Orleans, was designated to oversee the safe arrival of this shipment, while Dunn returned by ocean vessel to the United States.

The goods never arrived in Kentucky. A slow, soft crew wasted so much time working the boat up the river against the strong current that raw winter reached the Ohio River before they did. Their boat, frozen in, later sank with its expensive cargo of liquors, coffee, sugar, and linens. Wilkinson, who always searched for a scapegoat whenever he met failure, somehow managed to blame Clark for the loss, and later he canceled the trade agreement.

Nolan did not lose favor. Whatever his actions in the disaster, however, records have not disclosed them.

•

The loss of the boat heralded another turn in Wilkinson's fortunes. Although he continued to dispatch shipments to New Orleans and, for a while, to receive good Spanish money in payment, his star had begun to decline again. If the lost boat had been able to negotiate the upriver trip, as James R. Jacobs remarked in his biography, *Tarnished Warrior*, the partnership Wilkinson had formed with Clark and Dunn might have resulted in a close and lucrative Kentucky–New Orleans trade and cultural relationship. Instead, commerce and most other activity seemed destined now to be largely one way: down the river.

Nevertheless, Wilkinson still hoped he might find his fortune in the river trade. Anxious to maintain his cordial relationship with the Spaniards, he visited New Orleans again, in the summer of 1789, leaving his wife to mourn "the tedious hours" of his absence, as was so often her lot. In New Orleans he talked with Miró and with other Spaniards. Three months later he returned to Kentucky, with Nolan as his traveling companion, by way of the hazardous overland route — along the east bank of the Mississippi to Natchez, then along the densely wooded Natchez Trace into Tennessee, and finally to Kentucky. Fortunately, they escaped encounters with the bandits and Indians that lay in hiding, waiting to ambush the travelers of these roads.

Wilkinson and Nolan then arranged to dispatch still other tobacco shipments to New Orleans. By this time, however, talk of Wilkinson's precarious financial situation had become widespread throughout Kentucky; he owed for real estate and for tobacco. Obviously he was not the man of wealth many had presumed him to be, even though the Spaniards sent occasional payments to him for his tobacco.

Worse for him, even more damaging talk had been passed around. More people had begun to question Wilkinson's real motives in seeking independence for Kentucky. Some even claimed he was devoting himself solely to Spanish goals, for whatever reason. General Arthur St. Clair, governor of the Northwest Territory, wrote Wilkinson's associate — and St. Clair's former staff officer — Major Dunn, in December of 1788:

> I am much grieved to hear that there are strong dispositions on the part of the people of Kentucky to break off their connection with the United States, and that our friend Wilkinson is at the head of the affair. Such a consummation would involve the United States in the greatest difficulties, and would completely ruin this country. Should there be any foundation for these reports, for God's sake, make use of your influence to detach Wilkinson from that party.

Eight days later General St. Clair wrote another letter, to a government official in Philadelphia: "It is certain that, in the last convention [the Assembly seeking solutions for Kentucky problems], a proposal was made that the district of Kentucky should be set up for itself, not only independent of Virginia, but of the United States also, and was rejected by a small majority only."

Still other destructive gossip was to paint Wilkinson as an absolute scoundrel. In time he alienated certain individuals who knew something of his private life, and they whispered, correctly or not, that he was a paid Spanish agent, that the money coming up to him from New Orleans was in return for political services rendered to that foreign power. Wilkinson retorted, angrily, that all the money received had been due him for shipments of tobacco. He never once wavered, following his father's advice: "My son, if you ever put up with an insult I will disinherit you."

Whatever the truth was as to his Spanish connections, his financial difficulty became a fact. By early 1791 his indebtedness had risen to six thousand dollars — this against a man who always relished living and entertaining well — and it seemed certain to soar higher. To counteract this, he sent more tobacco to New Orleans; but his shipments, some of bad quality, already had flooded the market, and Governor Miró had grown cool toward further dealings. Nolan, who was in New Orleans at the time, sought to smooth the situation and, in fact, to expand the potential. On April 6, 1791, he wrote Wilkinson:

> ... I hope all your tobacco of this season will be admitted into the royal magazine. ...
>
> This day I will speak to the Governor and the Secretaries, about a contract for the supply of Mexico [meaning Texas] and if anything can be done, I will send an express through the woods. I have already mentioned it to Don Andre, but he gave me no hopes. I will, however, push the matter.
>
> ... I know not the language of compliment, but rest assured, your prosperity is intimately blended with the happiness of
>
> PHILIP NOLAN

The attempt proved to be unsuccessful. Later Miró told Wilkinson to stop all shipments.

Nevertheless, Wilkinson made one last effort to dispatch a cargo of tobacco. For this purpose, as it later developed, he formed a secret partnership with one Hugh McIlvaine, whose name was to be used solely in connection with the shipment. Wilkinson's letter of instruction to McIlvaine was found later.

McIlvaine was told to give out presents to the commandants of Spanish posts along the river, and to declare he had come to take an oath of allegiance to Spain. At New Orleans, McIlvaine was instructed to tell Governor Miró he had brought the tobacco — four hundred thousand pounds of it — for royal supplies, then to comment, without making too much of a show of it, that James Wilkinson realized the need for maintaining friendly relations and commercial intercourse with Spain, although some of Wilkinson's enemies in Kentucky — and they were named for McIlvaine's reference in the instructions — obviously did not realize this. Wilkinson added in his letter to McIlvaine, ". . . pay me any other Compliments you may think I deserve."

Even this effort did not save Wilkinson. With creditors hounding him, his lands and other property soon were to go on sale to pay his debts. Wilkinson cast about for some new catch and volunteered for a military campaign against the Indians. He was accepted as second-in-command and, in the spring of 1791, enjoyed considerable success, which he did not hesitate to publicize. Finally he was rewarded with an appointment by President Washington as lieutenant colonel in the United States Army. The appointment was dated October 22, 1791, at Philadelphia, where Wilkinson had admired the pomp and precision of the 18th Royal Irish Infantry eighteen years earlier.

5. VARYING FORTUNES

JAMES WILKINSON voiced his satisfaction in again taking up the sword of his country, but some of the pleasure no doubt stemmed from the easing of financial pressures against him.

Others were delighted, too. Wilkinson still had a loyal following in Kentucky. One important admirer remarked in a letter, "I flatter myself that the nation will find a valuable officer in Lt Col Wilkinson." The writer added that the recently commissioned colonel possessed youth, activity, ambition, and bravery, and said, ". . . he has always intimated to me that a military life was what he was anxious to attain to."

Wilkinson looked around, weighed his military attributes

with no lack of confidence, and foresaw a bright future, particularly since a superior officer, General St. Clair, the same man who had written Major Dunn of his fears regarding a Spanish "conspiracy," had run into difficulty in his campaign against the Indians.

St. Clair's troubles came from three sources: his own health, which was poor; his fellow citizens, who had no confidence in him; and the redmen themselves, who plagued his bedraggled army, then surprised and routed it in a 1791 battle — both tragic and embarrassing in its outcome — fought near the present site of Fort Wayne, Indiana. After St. Clair's eclipse, Wilkinson's sheen appeared even brighter, and the Colonel never permitted modesty to dim it. On March 5, 1792, Wilkinson received promotion to brigadier general.

For his military reincarnation Wilkinson's first post was Fort Washington, in Cincinnati, then a noisy frontier town of some one thousand inhabitants. The two hundred or so troops stationed there, many of them foreign born and in the army only because it served them as a haven, relieved their tedium by drinking, brawling with the citizens, and wenching — on a pay beginning at three dollars a month for privates — and Wilkinson's first task was to reestablish discipline. One remedy he generously prescribed was the whip. Drunkenness or fighting drew twenty-five or fifty lashes, but the threat of that cruel punishment still failed to discourage some army ruffians. If they could subsist on the scant daily ration of bread, meat, and whiskey — of which sometimes only the liquor was fit to swallow — they could survive anything, it seemed.

Wilkinson's officers apparently ranked only a notch or two above their men. Some were ignorant, almost illiterate. Many drank heavily and constantly. Wilkinson himself, however, contributed an air of civility to his post. He was well assisted by his gracious wife, who never failed to attract the admiration of Wilkinson's officers and even — to some lesser degree — of their wives. Together, the Wilkinsons gave banquets, balls, and parties, even on a pay of only three or four dollars a day, and their warm hospitality served to bolster the sagging morale.

A degree of tranquillity thus returned to the life of James Wilkinson. Although the General had found himself a new niche, however, his protégé Nolan now needed employment.

Not just any job would suit Nolan's temperament. He looked long and far — and westward, as Wilkinson had done eight years earlier, before moving to Kentucky. Westward now, however, meant even more challenge and peril, and, possibly, more opportunity than it had for Wilkinson. To Nolan, who had been dividing his time between New Orleans and Kentucky and perhaps places between, like Natchez, westward meant into what is now Texas.

Somewhere Nolan had heard of the wild horses that roamed the prairies and woodlands of that variegated region. Although he probably was not aware of it, they were offspring of horses brought to the Americas by the *conquistadores* — horses that had broken loose from their masters and found their own freedom in the New World. Possibly Nolan heard about their great numbers sometime while he was in New Orleans, acting as Wilkinson's agent. There he would have had an opportunity to become aware of a Royal Order of 1780, which permitted the importation of horses from Texas for marketing in Louisiana, where the animals were scarce.

Through the King's authorization, traders thus might obtain passports in New Orleans, travel into Texas with goods to exchange for horses, and return with the animals. Profits could be great, but the gambles matched them. The Spaniards could be as capricious in dealing with these traders as they had been in interfering with commerce on the Mississippi River.

Nolan was a young man who would have mulled over the money to be made through this trade. His letter of April 6, 1791, to Wilkinson (already quoted) had indicated that the two had been considering the chances of getting a contract "for the supply of Mexico" — which meant Texas, in view of Nolan's usage at that time — and this would have included plans for bringing horses back for sale in New Orleans, or anywhere else possible.

Now, with Wilkinson necessarily out of the picture, Nolan pursued the possibility of horse-trading the same way his erstwhile patron would have: he used his charm, and he used Wilkinson's name — plus a probable oath of allegiance to Spain — to get a passport from Governor Miró to go into Texas. He invested all he had in merchandise, no doubt borrowed more, and set out, expectantly, in the spring of 1791 for the faraway lands, with all his goods held in barrels carried on horseback.

Across the wind-rippled, shallow grass of Gulf plains he rode, through gloomy, moss-bannered woods. Occasionally he met Indians, made their friendly acquaintance, spoke to them in the sign language he had begun to master. He traded: for skins and furs, maybe for some wild horses the Indians had caught and tamed. He visited Nacogdoches, located deep in pine woods, established a friendship with a Spanish resident,

Antonio Leal, and his very amiable, inconstant wife, Gertrudis. He surely heard of, and possibly met, a Spaniard named Gil Antonio Ybarbo, known today as the founder of Nacogdoches.

From Ybarbo, Nolan could have learned a lesson that might have served him well later. Ybarbo, too, had sought riches in Nacogdoches, but a penchant for shrewd trading had contributed to his downfall. Appointed lieutenant governor, civil and military captain of militia, and judge of contraband, Ybarbo's power, exercised as it was so distant from surveillant Spanish authority, ran away with his self-control. The same year Nolan arrived in Nacogdoches, Ybarbo was accused of smuggling contraband goods into the town and, worse, of trading on the sly with Indians for horses stolen from his fellow Spaniards. Although Ybarbo was cleared of these charges, superiors doubted his integrity after that to such an extent that he was banished from the town for a number of years.

Nolan's own trading adventure collapsed about this time — perhaps because of a general suspicion aroused by Ybarbo's dealings — and another adventure, even more demanding, began for him.

Five years later Nolan was to write Wilkinson, on June 10, 1796, a brief description of what transpired during this period:

> Governor Miró informed you, that he had given me the necessary papers, for my security in Mexico [again, meaning Texas]. They did not answer his or my expectation, and I was soon spoken of as a spy. I was not imprisoned, but I was cheated out of all my goods, and in less than one year, reduced as poor as any Indian who roams the forest. Disappointed, distressed, tired of civilisation, and all its cares, I was about

to abandon it forever; the freedom, the independence of the
savage life was always cogenial to my nature, and I left the
Spaniards, and wandered among the Indians, that live between the Illinois [roughly, all the country north of where the
Yazoo River flowed into the Mississippi] and [San] Antonio;
this life, however, I found less pleasing in practice than speculation. I was a favourite with the Tawayes and Cam-
manches. . . .

No greater tribute to Nolan's eighteenth-century charm
and capacity could have been imagined than that he was a
favorite with the Comanches, who were then and later the
scourge of the Southwest, fighting with equal courage Spaniards, Mexicans, Anglo-Americans, and other Indian tribes.
Their name, in fact, came from a designation given them by
another tribe, and it meant "enemy."

Other Indians acknowledged Comanche supremacy in
many areas. Colonel Richard I. Dodge, who knew the characteristics of different tribes from personal observation, mentioned one instance:

> Where all are such magnificent thieves, it is difficult to
> decide which of the Plains tribes deserves the palm for steal-
> ing. The Indians themselves give it to the Comanches, whose
> designation in the sign language is a backward, wriggling
> motion of the index finger, signifying a snake, and indicating
> the silent stealth of that tribe. For crawling into a camp, cut-
> ting hopples and lariat ropes, and getting off undiscovered
> with the animals, they are unsurpassed and unsurpassable.

Nolan certainly could not have made himself a favorite
with these people, charm or not, without outstanding physical
ability and native intelligence. Comanches, especially after
they had acquired the horse, were active and aggressive; and
they possessed a powerful physique. Nolan's strength would

have impressed them: a story growing out of his days in Kentucky had it that he could, with one hand, lift off the back of a horse a bag containing two thousand dollars in coin of that day and carry it into Wilkinson's house.

Nolan was to become something of an authority on Indians. In his time with the Comanches he came to know them and their culture well. To these savages buffalo meant life itself; in their nomadic existence they spent much time tracking the animal which provided them with both food and clothing. Their acceptance of captives and other individuals into their tribal activities, including marriage, would have contributed to Nolan's easy integration in every respect while he was with them. Above all else, however, Comanche Indians were known on the frontier for their viciousness and for their ability to attack, to steal, to kill, and to vanish before their pursuers could locate them. Early Spaniards had foreseen what the horse might do for savages like these and had forbidden them to own, or even to ride, that animal, but the order was no longer enforceable.

From the Comanches, or from some other tribe, Nolan probably learned the various methods of capturing wild horses, a tricky and often cruel activity, especially as the Indians practiced it. In its simplest technique, as described by J. Frank Dobie in *The Mustangs*, it worked this way: after lassoing the animal they "choked it down" by tightening the lariat over the windpipe. When the horse had dropped to the ground, frothing in frenzy and apparently about to choke to death, they grabbed the head, tied the feet, then slackened the lariat, allowing the horse to breathe again. Then they allowed the animal to become accustomed to their smell: wild horses were as alert in smelling as they were in seeing, and strange odors disturbed them greatly. No wild horse felt acquainted with any object until he had smelled it.

The Indians' treatment broke some horses sufficiently for the savages to ride them, but others required still more persuasion. On these the Indians used a hackamore or a hobble, or some other method of restricting the horse's movements until it had become accustomed to its new life and to its owners. "These horses . . . are caught in a most curious manner," said an Englishman to whom Nolan once described the techniques, "and which can only be effected with success by those who have been used to the practice."

After two years with the Indians, Nolan found the life "less pleasing in practice than speculation," as he later wrote Wilkinson.

> . . . I could not altogether Indianfy my heart; — the ties that bound me to society, memory supported — I was a debtor — I had been the only hope of a fond parent — Morality at length prevailed, and after two years lost, in these savage wanderings, I returned to the Spaniards, determined to make another exertion. — I shall not at present intrude on your attention, by a minute recital of my little adventures. I turned hunter; sold skins; caught wild horses, and made my way to Louisiana, with 50 head. At Orleans, I was received as a person risen from the dead. . . .

Nolan surely was as glad to see New Orleans as his astonished friends were to see him upon his miraculous return from Texas, in 1794, after three years. The city had been rebuilt after the disastrous 1788 fire, and had, in fact, survived two others, neither of which had caused so much damage because of the application of lessons learned from the earlier disaster. Residents were as fun-loving as ever, and the Creole cooking seemed as succulent: assorted game and gumbos that were to be found only in New Orleans, all accompanied by the appropriate choice wines. That year the first newspaper, *Le Moniteur de la Louisiane*, began publishing — in the French language, of course — and the first highly profitable sugar-cane crop was harvested at a plantation six miles above the city.

Upon his return, Nolan, having an attentive eye for feminine beauty, surely would have noticed the women of New Orleans society. Virtually all of them were brunettes, and their complexions were delicate and fetching: this he would have perceived even through their veils. None of these ladies walked; many of them rode, alone, in chair carriages. Nolan was not a man of sufficient social standing to attract any of them.

Certainly these ladies would not condescend to walk the unpaved New Orleans streets after the frequent rains, which left the black loam looking like a layer of grease. After these downpours, the unlucky pedestrians walked down a long, tight bridge of single logs placed end to end, the only sidewalk available in those days.

Nolan learned that a new governor had replaced Miró: the Baron de Carondelet; and he soon arranged to meet him. Carondelet proved to be a sympathetic, though rather ordinary, administrator. Already he had effected some improvements and would institute others: under his guidance came the first lighting of streets (eighty lamps at first); the first civilian night watchmen (thirteen initially), who regularly called out hours and the state of the weather in addition to guarding against malfeasance. Slaves were more liberally treated: by Carondelet's order Sunday became their free day, and at no time could any of them be given punishment greater than twenty-five lashes. Still better, for Nolan, was Caron-delet's generosity in approving a passport for his return to Texas. This permit was not intended as a carte blanche for trading, which was still ostensibly prohibited, but Nolan anticipated no difficulty in his forthcoming venture.

By June 6, 1794, he had returned to Nacogdoches, accom-panied by five Louisiana citizens and a Negro slave. This secluded village, which Nolan already knew intimately by now, had been planted by the Spaniards deep in the red-soil and pine-tree region of what is now East Texas. A mission had been established there in 1716 for the dual purpose of baptizing the reluctant Indians into Catholicism, an endeavor which failed early, and of fending off unwanted foreign traders — as this man Nolan would prove to be — an en-deavor which also failed eventually. For a time the site had been abandoned to the Indians, and the residents had been removed to San Antonio, but in 1779 the Spaniard Gil Antonio Ybarbo, whose perfidious trading techniques would bring his downfall twelve years after this date, had brought the colony back to "the site of the Tejas Indians," as he wrote in a letter, "and three leagues beyond, the old mission of Nacogdoches, where there was a small chapel, where the reverend father may perform the holy sacraments and a house where he may live, as well as plenty of water, lands, and materials for houses."

The village, whose population numbered five hundred when Nolan returned there in 1794, had grown up near the mission, Nuestra Señora de Guadalupe de Nacogdoches, in rolling forest land watered by clear, cool streams, inhabited by friendly, agrarian Indians of the Hasinai confederation of Caddo, and supplied with abundant game — bear, deer, buffalo, squirrel, wild turkey, fish — plenty to keep a table full. Despite its remoteness, it was inevitably linked to the rest of the Spanish empire by a ribbon of a trail, El Camino Real, one of several roads with such designations blazed in the Spanish New World. This one had been laid out in 1691 by Domingo Terán de los Rios, the first provincial governor of Texas, to connect his capital at Monclova, in Coahuila, Mexico, with missions established among the Indians of this area. It wound through a varied landscape: from the sun-baked earth to the west, into a hillocky central region, and finally, after wearying weeks of travel, through well-watered thickets at the eastern end. Probably the road followed an old Indian trail, possibly the same one that the French explorer La Salle had once traveled and had found "as well beaten a road as that from Paris to Orléans."

Nacogdoches, despite its isolation, was a busy village, crowded on fiesta days with townspeople, Indians, farmers, traders, and soldiers, with uniformed men and with robed priests whose presence rarely curtailed the excesses of the army. Narrow, red-dirt streets lined with frame buildings led to the most imposing structure in the village: a large stone house, with walls a yard thick, which had been built by Ybarbo around 1779 as a commissary for storing merchandise.

A few years after he had built the stone house, the same Ybarbo, before being deposed of all his esteemed offices, had granted Nolan's acquaintances, Antonio and Gertrudis Leal, a four-league-square tract of land located at the present site of San Augustine, Texas. Now, during his 1794 trip, Nolan solidified his friendship with the Leals — whose ranch he sometimes used to pasture his horses — and particularly with Gertrudis, who became his mistress. They made a strange triangle: Nolan's age was twenty-three; Gertrudis', forty-three; and Antonio's, fifty-two. Adding to the peculiarity was Antonio Leal's attitude. He seemed not to object to the arrangement: even after its consummation he remained on good terms with Nolan, and, in fact, worked closely with him, as with a brother.

Nolan also made enemies at Nacogdoches. One of them was a fellow Irishman, William Barr, later the possessor of a royal license to trade with the Indians. He resented Nolan, and particularly the competition Nolan represented, although for the moment the two maintained a peaceable, if not cordial, relationship. Neither man could abide the other for long, however, and their truce was not to last.

Mostly, the trip was pleasant. This time the Spaniards honored Nolan's passport, and they winked at the trading, as it was their custom to do when they felt so inclined.

From Nacogdoches Nolan traveled farther westward, in December of that year, to San Antonio, the Spanish capital of Texas, whose two thousand residents — including the military — seemed entirely too many for the land to support, notwithstanding the richness of soil along the banks of a river that ran through the city. A letter written by a Spanish official around that time described the situation. The many potential benefits of San Antonio had not been realized, he said, because of the general poverty of the area. The inhabitants, lacking both means and energy, planted vegetable crops sufficient only for their own use. Arts, industry, and other agriculture were absent. Only the availability of buffalo, which were hunted from May to October, and of wild mustangs, which were also sought and frequently eaten instead of ridden after capture, kept some people alive.

At San Antonio Nolan presented himself to Governor
Muñoz and, as usual in these situations, made himself pleasant. He sought permission to engage in trade, for in no other
way could he get horses quickly. Obviously the answer was
affirmative or, more likely, a figurative wink and a smile.
Muñoz might even have acquired a share in the enterprise.
Certainly he was aware of Nolan's purpose, as one of his
letters shows. Writing to the commandant at Nacogdoches
on March 12, 1795, Muñoz declared:

> . . . all this you must read and keep between yourself and our
> friend Guadiana. Nothing must get out except what you tell
> Nolan to guide him in the matter, so that he may know that
> you are making a confidant of him. He must not confide in
> anyone, and, especially, the people of Nacogdoches.

Nolan himself had apparently embarked on some intrigues
of his own about this time. Since he had traveled widely
across Texas — farther, it developed later, than the Spaniards
themselves realized — he knew the region better than any
other Anglo-American and, in fact, better than the Spaniards.
He had acquired sufficient knowledge to make some rough
maps of Texas, and if these lacked accuracy, as it seemed they
did, at least they existed, at a time when maps were scarce.
Amos Stoddard, an early nineteenth-century writer, referred
to one of them:

> The adventurer, Philip Nolan, who visited the borders of
> New Mexico [meaning Texas] about the year 1796, . . . con-
> structed a map of one of his tours, on which he delineated a
> salt mountain, and beneath the delineation wrote *"here your
> friend encamped three weeks."* The gentleman, to whom he
> presented the map, questioned him relative to what appeared

a phenomenon, and he declared with the strongest asseveration, that a mountain of fossil salt actually existed a little to the southward of the sources of Red river. This map has been inspected by the author . . . [Stoddard].

Nolan probably did not visit the salt mountain in 1796, however, because in either late 1795 or early 1796 he returned to the United States. On June 10, 1796, he wrote General Wilkinson the letter, already quoted, in which he referred to his two-year wandering among the Indians. Now, in that same letter, he brought his former patron up to date with details of his trip just ended. "Returned again to St. Antonio [in 1794]," he wrote, "and purchased and caught 250 head [of wild horses]. I lost a great part of those by the *yellow water*; sold the best at Natchez, and arrived here yesterday with 42 head."

> I lament [he continued], there is none of these worthy of your saddle. I had one, I had called your charger, as white as snow, all obedience, but was the first carried off by that cursed distemper. I shall, however, take over a dark bay, 5 years old, well broke; and next spring, bring you one fit for a warrior.
>
> So soon as I can get your's, and one to ride in tolerable order, I will visit you. In the mean time, present me affectionately to Mrs. Wilkinson and Biddle, and believe me to be, sincerely, your's,
>
> PHILIP NOLAN

During the five years since Nolan had last written Wilkinson, and since Wilkinson had concluded his commercial ventures with the Spaniards, he, like Nolan, had experienced varying fortunes and moods. For much of that time he had served as second-in-command on the northwestern frontier under haughty General Anthony Wayne, who had been sent with orders to effect a peace with the Indians, preferably by treaty, but by force if necessary. Supporting the Indians against the Americans, not surprisingly, were the British, who maintained forts in the region around Canada.

Neither of the American officers cared for the other. Wilkinson disliked Wayne, a man of great frankness, and no doubt he envied him his rank. Once he wrote the Secretary of War a letter declaring that Wayne was incompetent, a charge he later withdrew. Wayne, on the other hand, could not stomach Wilkinson's deviousness, which had become obvious to him if not to some others, and he neither respected nor trusted his second-in-command. Frequently, it seemed — to Wilkinson at least — Wayne ignored him during campaigns.

At the Battle of Fallen Timbers, fought near a British fort in a tornado-swept forest clearing fifteen miles from what is now Toledo, Ohio, Wayne won a victory over the Indians that showed them they could not regard the British as being very staunch allies: when the savages fled toward the fort the Englishmen kept the gates closed, and the Indians were forced to race on through the forest to escape.

The battle also won for Wayne the thanks of Congress, but not the thanks of Wilkinson. Although Wayne had singled out his second-in-command for commendation in his post-battle report, Wilkinson continued to berate his commander in private conversation and correspondence, and to criticize Wayne's handling of the entire operation against the Indians. Finally, when Wilkinson realized that the public worshiped Wayne as a hero for his campaign against the Indians, he ceased his attacks, to avoid a showdown with such a popular man, but he continued to plot Wayne's ruin.

As for Wayne, he made little effort now to disguise the blackest suspicions of Wilkinson. He suggested that Wilkinson resign, since he was a paper general only and had no troops to lead, but Wayne probably entertained no hope that his pompous subordinate would take his advice. Equally embarrassing for Wilkinson, Wayne at this time had begun to suspect that the Spaniards in New Orleans were up to some devilment in regard to the United States, and he brought out of storage past rumors of Wilkinson's involvement.

Thomas Power, a man Wayne felt sure was a Spanish agent, had been in the area recently to visit Wilkinson. Wayne's suspicions were thoroughly aroused by this and other occurrences, and he ordered all boats coming up the Mississippi River to be searched. Apparently he heard a report about this time — and passed it on to the War Department — that Wilkinson's former assistant, Philip Nolan, newly returned to Kentucky from New Orleans, had received from Power a sum of nine thousand dollars, in behalf of Wilkinson. Then, abruptly, a shroud was dropped over all of Wayne's worries. His health, weakened by wounds and other vicissitudes of his long service, gave out. On a cold December day in 1796 he died, and James Wilkinson became ranking general in the Western Country.

Ironically, Wilkinson could not be as delighted as he might have been at the unexpected good fortune; his heart was burdened with grief at this time. He and Mrs. Wilkinson had recently completed a voyage up the Ohio River to Pittsburgh, thence overland to Philadelphia, where they planned to visit their sons John and James, in school there, and to enjoy a vacation from the rigors of frontier life. Upon their arrival at Pittsburgh on October 20, however, they learned that John had died during their slow river trip, and their anticipated delight at seeing Philadelphia had palled.

6. A DECEPTIVE GAME

WHEN GENERAL AND MRS. WILKINSON reached Pittsburgh en route to Philadelphia, they happened to meet a well-known surveyor, Andrew Ellicott, who was on his way south toward Natchez to serve as an American commissioner in determining a firm boundary between the United States and Spanish Florida, in accordance with a recently signed Treaty of San Lorenzo between the United States and Spain.

That agreement also defined certain other relationships between the two countries and guaranteed American use of the Mississippi River — and New Orleans as a place of deposit for commercial goods — for the next three years. In accordance with its terms, the Spaniards also would evacuate forts at Natchez and elsewhere along the east bank of the Mississippi north of latitude thirty-one degrees. This previously disputed territory would pass into United States control.

Wilkinson offered the use of his boat for the trip downriver, and Ellicott accepted quickly and gratefully: the General traveled in style, he knew, and the boat cabin was spacious.

Wilkinson might have had another reason for offering the vessel besides the fact that Ellicott was a fellow official serving the United States. The surveyor had just left the seat of government, Philadelphia, where Wayne recently had been raising fresh questions about Wilkinson's integrity. Furthermore, Ellicott was bound for Wilkinson country, where he would no doubt hear other gossip of the General's disloyalty. Throughout the entire period Ellicott would be in continual communication with Philadelphia, because of his work. Considering the situation, it seemed wise for Wilkinson to cultivate a most amicable relationship with Ellicott, a conclusion that might help explain the reason for Philip Nolan's supposedly chance encounter with Ellicott, too, although Nolan had a legitimate reason for being where he was.

The two met "at the confluence of the Ohio and Mississippi" rivers, where Ellicott's party of thirty men, including an army escort, arrived in late December 1796, after navigating down the cold Ohio from Pittsburgh with three other boats besides the one borrowed from Wilkinson. Air temperatures had ranged between twenty and thirty-five degrees for most of the trip, and the river temperature stood at thirty-three degrees. At the junction of the Mississippi and the Ohio both rivers became so jammed with ice Ellicott was forced to stop. He had not expected such cold weather.

Unfortunately, a "stores" boat containing essentials like blankets and other gear had not been able to keep up with the rest; so when they encamped, on December 22, they lit large fires and kept the flames roaring day and night, for warmth. From the frozen rivers came a rumbling "like an earthquake": the ice, all in motion, was grinding and crashing together.

At this time Philip Nolan, recently returned from a mapping expedition up the Missouri River, strode into Ellicott's camp, en route from New Madrid to Fort Massac, which was located a short distance farther up the Ohio River, in what is now Illinois. Two boats in Nolan's charge had been frozen in earlier at Massac, and the young Irishman "known for his athletic exertions," as Ellicott wrote in his journal, was going to investigate their situation.

His willingness to socialize, however, persuaded Nolan to stop in Ellicott's camp, and he soon captivated Ellicott with his stories of adventure in Texas. Nolan related something of his experiences with the Indians and with the wild horses; and once, when he saw a group of Indians nearing Ellicott's camp, Nolan called out a greeting to them. When it became obvious they had not understood him, he switched to sign language, and they answered him at once. Ellicott, standing nearby, was fascinated by the exchange: this was the first time he had seen sign language used.

Nolan seemed to know a great deal about many things. "From him I obtained much useful information relative to the situations and characters of the principal inhabitants of Natchez," Ellicott wrote, "which at that time was a matter of mere curiosity but which eventually I found extremely useful." Probably, too, Nolan was able to interject a good word or two for Wilkinson; the General's associates had a habit of doing this when it mattered.

"Being pleased with his conversation," Ellicott continued,

"and finding that he had a very extensive knowledge of that country, particularly Louisiana, I requested the pleasure of his company down the river, as we were unacquainted with the navigation of it." In return, Ellicott said he would instruct Nolan in astronomy and navigation and map-making, subjects in which Nolan expressed interest and already possessed some ability. Nolan agreed to go, but said he must first look after his two boats. While he was at Massac, he said, he would also investigate the whereabouts of Ellicott's supply boat.

The morning after Nolan's arrival in camp he proceeded to Massac and remained there until Ellicott's tardy boat arrived; then, when the ice permitted, he brought all three boats downstream and rejoined Ellicott, on January 29. By that time the weather had moderated, and a temporary rise on both rivers had helped to carry off the ice. The next day they repacked, and on January 31 they set off, in a chilly rain that was to be a harbinger of the voyage.

Trouble first developed two days later at New Madrid, a Spanish post on the west bank of the Mississippi from which Nolan had only recently departed when he encountered Ellicott. At New Madrid the Americans were received cordially enough — artillery saluted their arrival and officers of the garrison greeted them respectfully — but during the conversation that evening the post commandant casually suggested to Ellicott that he remain at New Madrid for two or three days. When Ellicott refused, the commandant summoned him into a private room, called for an Irish priest to interpret, and explained to Ellicott a dilemma. Governor Carondelet, the commandant said, had given orders that Ellicott not be allowed to descend the Mississippi until the Spanish posts on the east bank had been evacuated in accordance with the treaty. These posts could not be evacuated until the river rose with the spring floods, usually about April, the commandant added.

Ellicott replied that the order seemed "extraordinary" to him, that the depth of the river at that very time was sufficient to allow evacuation, and that Carondelet's order violated the treaty. In any event, he added, he could not delay any longer; already he had lagged behind schedule.

At four o'clock in the afternoon of the day after he arrived Ellicott persistently ordered his men into their boats, pushed off, and proceeded two miles down the river where they camped. Free of the Spaniards' surveillance, he mused over Carondelet's orders until late in the evening. Probably he discussed the situation with Nolan, since he had been asking Nolan's advice in various matters, but this was not recorded. Nolan would have been an interested, and perhaps amused, listener.

At Chickasaw Bluffs, near Memphis, another Spanish commandant received them amiably, five days after their departure from New Madrid. At this post, however, no one — neither the commandant nor his officers — seemed to be acquainted with the treaty under which Ellicott claimed to be operating, and Ellicott saw no indication whatsoever that the Spaniards planned to evacuate their fort.

He now became more alarmed than ever and discussed his fears with Nolan, who sought at once to quiet him. "Keep your suspicions to yourself," Nolan said, according to Ellicott in his journal. "By no means let them appear, you may depend upon me, whatever I can discover, you shall know, but the utmost caution will be necessary, both for your success, and my own safety."

If Nolan discovered anything, however, he must have kept it to himself, because Ellicott, in the journal, recorded no information as having come from him. Instead, Nolan probably listened intently to all conversations and filed the knowledge for possible future use. He liked to keep informed of the latest happenings.

Two days after their arrival, Ellicott's party left Chickasaw Bluffs. After their departure the weather grew more unpleasant: gales and rainstorms frequently sent them scurrying for the shore, where lightning flickered over their hastily erected tents and thunderclaps kept them awake. Even during the few quiet periods relaxation was difficult. Alligators along the banks occasionally startled them; some unseasonably warm, damp weather proved uncomfortable and brought thick fog; and the everlasting mosquitoes attacked them unmercifully. At one point they were detained for an hour by two Spanish galleys.

On February 19 they arrived at Walnut Hills, or Nogales, near where Vicksburg stands today. There, on a "handsome and commanding" height, the Spaniards maintained a strong fortification, but the surroundings appeared peaceful enough. Ellicott remarked on the beauty of the place: transplanted peach trees bloomed on the hills, the maples had begun to green in the seventy-nine-degree weather, a hint of an early spring appeared everywhere. Nearby, a small but picturesque stream cascaded from the hills into the river below.

The water, however, was of bad quality, the commandant declared, and the climate not healthful. To Ellicott the entire atmosphere, in fact, seemed ominous: they had been summoned to shore in the first place by a discharge of Spanish artillery, although they were making for the landing at the time; and this commandant, too, appeared to be ignorant of the treaty that brought the Americans there.

Soon after landing, Ellicott and Nolan had called on the commandant. When the Spaniard voiced ignorance of the treaty, Ellicott, exasperated but not surprised, sent to his boat for a copy.

The commandant's manner was, however, urbane in the best Spanish tradition. He entertained them sumptuously and provided a conducted tour of his post, but Ellicott kept on his guard. After a one-day visit he resumed the trip with characteristic resoluteness, but on the following day a canoe from Nogales overtook him with this message, which had arrived at the post overland from Manuel Gayoso, then commandant at Natchez, and had been dispatched immediately to Ellicott:

> . . . It is with pleasure that I propose myself the satisfaction of seeing you here and [making] your acquaintance.
>
> Though I do not conceive that the least difficulty will arise respecting the execution of the part of the treaty in which you are an acting person, yet as we are not prepared to evacuate the posts immediately for want of the vessels that I expect will arrive soon, I find it indispensable to request you to leave the troops about the mouth of Bayou [Pierre], where they may be provided with all their necessaries, which you can regulate on your arrival here. By this means every unforeseen misunderstanding will be prevented between his Majesty's troops and those of the United States, besides it is necessary to make some arrangements previously to the arrival of the troops, of which subject I shall have the honour of entertaining you when we meet. . . .

Ellicott now felt sure that difficulties would ensue, and he was correct. After leaving his army escort at Bayou Pierre, a one-day voyage above Natchez, he arrived at his destination on February 24, and sent a message by Nolan to Gayoso:

Landing at the Town of Natchez, Feb. 24th, 1797

Sir,

It is with pleasure that I announce to you, my arrival as commissioner on behalf of the United States, for carrying into effect the third article of the treaty lately concluded between the said United States, and his Catholic Majesty.

I wish to be informed, when it will be convenient for your Excellency to receive my credentials.

I am, sir, with due respect,
Your humble servant,
ANDREW ELLICOTT

The reply, insolent in its brevity, was delivered that evening by Gayoso's secretary.

Natchez, 24th Feb. 1797.

Sir,

By your favour of this day, delivered to me by Mr. Nolan, I learn with pleasure your arrival at this post, in the character of commissionary in behalf of the United States, to ascertain the boundaries between the Territory of his most Catholic Majesty, and that of the said United States.

I have the honour to be, with the highest respect,
Sir, your most humble servant,
MANUEL GAYOSO DE LEMOS

The absence of any word about presentation of credentials upset Ellicott and heralded weeks of bickering. Even though he did indeed meet Gayoso the next day, February 25, the situation deteriorated rapidly after that. Ellicott hoisted the United States flag over his encampment, located at the "upper end of town" a quarter of a mile from the Spanish fort, and

Gayoso sent his messenger requesting the colors be lowered. Ellicott refused, and the flag stayed up. Nolan observed these displays of nationalism, but apparently kept his feelings to himself.

About this time Ellicott heard that Gayoso had written a letter to someone saying that Spain never intended to carry the treaty into effect; and, in fact, Ellicott recorded in his journal that the letter had been in his hands. He wrote also that he had heard rumors of the territory's impending cession to France. Adding to all this unpleasantness, a party of Indians encamped nearby became insolent one night and at the height of a drunken revelry threatened to attack the Americans. Ellicott prevailed upon his esteemed friend Nolan to quiet them, and he did so. Thereafter, Nolan said later, he stayed with the distraught Ellicott for two days in an attempt to calm him. For future safety Ellicott brought his military escort down from Bayou Pierre, and Gayoso let this affront pass.

Letters dripping with false courtesy passed between Gayoso and Ellicott. The American insisted vehemently, but politely, that the boundary survey begin; Gayoso continued to present sugary excuses for postponing it. The alibis continued to be much the same from letter to letter, until, one day, Ellicott read a new one: war had broken out between Spain and Great Britain, and Gayoso stated that an impending British attack, aimed down the Mississippi from Canada, threatened Spanish posts. Instead of evacuation, Gayoso declared, reinforcement would be necessary.

Eventually, however, the Spaniards gave in, and Andrew Ellicott began his long, arduous survey of the boundary between the United States and Spanish Florida, which included the exhausting task of hacking out a clearing sixty feet wide from the Mississippi River eastward to Georgia.

Ellicott performed still another service for his country, one of espionage. As General Wilkinson surely had anticipated, Ellicott was reporting to Philadelphia all rumors of intrigue he heard on the frontier, but Wilkinson was perhaps ignorant of the fact that Washington himself had requested Ellicott to report on Wilkinson's activites.

Unknown also to Wilkinson, at least at the time, was the fact that his name appeared in two damaging reports.

Within a year or so after Ellicott's arrival at Natchez he was to dispatch several communications to the State Department, but none of them was regarded seriously enough to arouse action; the Secretary of State believed, correctly, that the fantastic schemes detailed by Ellicott were incapable of success. The first letter was written and sent in the summer of 1797; in it Ellicott warned that Thomas Power, whom General Wayne had singled out earlier as a Spanish agent, was en route to visit Wilkinson, then in Detroit. In another letter, sent to Philadelphia in cipher but reproduced in plain language in Ellicott's journal, he wrote of a daring plot:

Natchez, Nov. 14th, 1798

Shortly after the ratification of the late treaty between the U.S. and his Catholic Majesty was carried to Kentucky, Mr. Murray an attorney at law in that State proceeded down the Mississippi to visit Govr Gayoso and the Baron de Carondelet. A few days after Mr. Murry's [sic] interview Mr. [Thomas] Power was despatched up the river apparently upon a trading voyage. He had secreted in a [barrel] of sugar four despatches in cipher one was directed to Genl Wilkinson, another to John Brown Senator of U.S. the third to Judge Sebastian, and the fourth to Mr. Lackasang at the rapids of the Ohio. These four men and Mr. Murry receive annual stipends from the Crown of Spain and several others whose names I have not learned receive occasional payments. Mr. Power delivered the despatches above mentioned himself. He met Gen. Wilkinson at Cincinnati in September last was a year. They affected for some days to be upon bad terms but were privately closeted at night.

This correspondence in cipher has been carried on for several years, it is ingeniously managed, the letters are deciphered by a pocket dictionary.

The first object of these plotters is to detach the States of Kentucky and Tenesee [sic] from the union and place them under the protection of Spain. If that could have been effected this season the treaty would never have been carried into effect: and to ascertain the probability of such an event, Mr. Power was sent in the beginning of last June into the States before mentioned.

The decision of detaching the western country from the union is but a small part of the general plan which is very extensive and embraces objects of immense magnitude; nevertheless, to insure success, this point must be first carried; which being effected and by the system of promotion adopted by the court of Madrid, Govr Gayoso will be at Quito and the Baron de Carondelet at Mexico about the same time: so soon as this arrangement takes place or sooner if the necessary officers can be corrupted a general insurrection will be attempted, and cannot fail of success if the first part succeeds. Gen¹ Wilkinson is to proceed from Kentucky with a body of troops through the country by the way of the Illinois into New Mexico [Texas] which will be a central position — the route has been already explored. Nine-tenths of the officers of the Louisiana regiment are at this time corrupted and the officers of the Mexican regiment which is now in this country are but little better. The apparent zeal of the Spanish officers on the Mississippi for the dignity of the crown, is only intended to cover their designs till the great plan which is the establishment of a new empire is brought to maturity. Their principles are highly revolutionary. This being understood the policy of the present Spanish Governors in this country in enticing our citizens to settle under their juris-

diction may be easily discovered. From the manner by which I
have obtained the forementioned information (which I am convinced is correct) I am unable to make any other use of it than to
communicate it to our first magistrate and the department of state
that the plan so far as it affects the United States may be counter-
acted — it must remain secret.

ELLICOTT

Ellicott realized that Nolan and Wilkinson were closely
associated, but if he ever wrote a public or private incrimina-
tion of Nolan the document has not been found.

Instead he did just the opposite. He always spoke highly of
Nolan's integrity and reliability, and he gave Nolan a pair of
field glasses and a good timepiece for making navigational
observations. All this he did even though he once received
intelligence that might have caused him to question the character of his riverboat companion. In April or early May, 1797,
at the peak of Ellicott's dispute with Gayoso at Natchez —
and sometime after Nolan had quieted the drunken Indians
— Nolan traveled down the Mississippi to New Orleans to
show Governor Carondelet the maps he had made of the
Missouri River country, to suggest that he be allowed to
survey Texas similarly, and to request a passport to go there
for this purpose and for his own commercial ventures.

Ellicott heard about Nolan's interview with Carondelet
through a confidential channel, and he recorded it in his
journal. Apparently he did not believe it, or, if he did, he did
not take it seriously.

> . . . [Nolan] had at different times been much favored by
> the Spanish government, particularly in being permitted to
> take and dispose of wild horses which are to be found in vast
> numbers west of the Mississippi and from his singular address
> and management had much of the governor general the Baron

de Carondelet's confidence who informed him . . . that the troubles were becoming serious up the river but that he was determined to quiet them by giving the Americans lead and the inhabitants [of Natchez, who were also troubling Gayoso] hemp and asked Mr. Nolan if he would take an active part in the expedition to which he replied, "A very active one."

The knowledge of it was kept from the inhabitants of the district first because its being known would injure, if not ruin, Mr. Nolan, and a few others, and secondly, had it been made public, it would have been impossible to restrain some of the inhabitants from committing hostilities.

Years later Ellicott was to reiterate his belief in Nolan. "I do not recollect to have ever received a hint, that . . . Mr. P. Nolan was concerned in any plans or intrigue injurious to the United States. On the contrary, in all our private and confidential conversations, he appeared strongly attached to the interest and welfare of our country."

Ellicott was to be questioned later about his impression of Nolan, especially in regard to Nolan's association with Wilkinson, whom Ellicott had accused in the letter to the Department of State of being a paid Spanish agent.

Q. What was [Nolan's] general character, and did he not render you services on your route down the Mississippi, to Natchez, as commissioner of limits?

A. Nolan's general character was good, as far as he [Ellicott] knew, and . . . he rendered essential services, during the mission.

Q. Was he not zealously attached to the United States, and do you not think he would have supported, in the interest of the United States, at every hazard of life and property, against any power whatever?

A. Affirmative.

Q. Did you ever converse with him, respecting General Wilkinson's connexion and intercourse, with the Spanish government of

Louisiana? State every thing concerning the same; whether the
said Nolan did not explain to your satisfaction, the nature of that
intercourse to be commercial, and whether you have not expressed
this circumstance to others?

A. To the . . . interrogatory, he answers, that he is strongly
inclined to believe, that Nolan mentioned to him, that the intercourse and connexion of General Wilkinson was commercial; and
that this made considerable impression on his mind; but he cannot
recollect, whether or not he has expressed this circumstance to
others.

Q. Did not the said Nolan inform you, that General Wilkinson
had been playing, a deceptive game with the Spaniards and do you
not know, that a deceptive policy and fictitious appearances, were
necessary, with the Spanish government, to protect Nolan's political or commercial enterprises in Louisiana?

A. To the . . . interrogatory, he answers in the negative, so far
as respects General Wilkinson; but that Nolan had told him that
a deceptive policy, and fictitious appearances were necessary on his
part to protect his enterprise in Louisiana.

Q. Did he ever communicate to you any plan he had projected,
to save the district of Natchez, if it had been attacked by the Baron
of Carondelet, by seizing that officer, when on a reconnoitering
party, and bearing him off to the people of the district?

A. To the . . . interrogatory, he answers in the affirmative; and
that he had made a communication on that subject, to the department of state.

Ellicott might have been less trusting of Nolan had he
known about an exchange of letters between Nolan and
Gayoso in Natchez little more than three weeks after Ellicott's
arrival there for the boundary survey. Gayoso, who of course
knew that Nolan had gone on expeditions into Texas with
Governor Carondelet's permission, evidently became per-
plexed about Nolan's close association with the American surveyor. On March 13, 1797, when Ellicott had begun showing

the United States colors at his camp despite Gayoso's dis-
approval, Gayoso addressed from his Natchez headquarters
a query to "Mr. Philip Noland."

"What political interest do you embrace?" he asked, "and
what interest do you regard with indifference or for which you
would take an active part?"

"Spain," Nolan answered in a reply dated in Natchez the
same day, written in his own hand, and on the same paper as
Gayoso's query, "& properly encouraged would take an *active
part* not as negociator but a *warrior*."

Gayoso did not quite understand the meaning of Nolan's
last sentence and queried him again. Nolan answered:

> . . . When I said that I would be employed as a *Warrior*
> and not a *Negociator* I meant that I would do what is honour-
> able and detest every thing mean. — He that is capable to
> betray even the confidence of an Enemy — is unworthy your
> protection or esteem, and I lament that y^r. Excellency has
> misunderstood me. —
>
> I will take the first opportunity to inform M^r. Ellicott that
> I am a Spaniard and that the part I have already acted was
> with a view to promote the interest of both countries.
>
> If your Excellency thinks proper to employ me against the
> British on the Missouri, or any other enterprise that may be
> honourable I flatter myself you will find your confidence not
> misplaced. . . .

7. DANGEROUS MEN

ON SEPTEMBER 27, 1798, General James Wilkinson, ranking officer in the United States Army, arrived in Natchez to
establish his headquarters on the frontier, where he had been
ordered to work toward a firm peace with the Spaniards and
with the Indians.

He came in a glow of success, having just pacified some
Indians along the Ohio. For this triumph he relied on substantial gifts for the savages, bought with federal money, rea-
soning that this was cheaper than fighting an Indian war, and
on elimination of cheating by the whites who had contact
with the Indians.

For a time before his arrival, war between the United States and Spain had threatened, as it was to do from time to time until the Spanish-American War a century later. Finally, however, the Spaniards had withdrawn from their forts along the Mississippi, including Natchez, in keeping with the terms of the recently signed treaty. At Natchez this had necessitated only a move westward across the river, which was still Spanish territory.

Ellicott had begun his work on the boundary survey, and in August the United States had dispatched dour Winthrop Sargent to Natchez as governor of the Mississippi Territory.

Wilkinson was careful to maintain friendly relations with both Ellicott and Sargent — at least at this time — and since Mrs. Wilkinson and their sons had remained at Fort Washington temporarily, the General had time on his hands for socializing with them. Neither Ellicott nor Sargent was well liked in Natchez, a fact that accorded a certain advantage in the relationship to the popular — if not thoroughly trusted — Wilkinson, who was as careful to maintain cordial relations, too, with the Spaniards nearby.

The Wilkinson charm still worked. Ellicott came to consider him such a good friend that he informed the General of the sinister reports he had been receiving regarding his loyalty — and that he considered them false, designed to ruin Wilkinson's reputation. Evidently he did not add that he had forwarded the intelligence to Philadelphia.

Wilkinson apparently remained calm and not much concerned about what Ellicott told him. He continued with his work, which included not only the peace efforts, but the construction of a fort near what was then the southwestern extremity of the United States. At this site men and supplies were to be gathered in force for the strategic border area, and from here the activities of the Spaniards might be kept under surveillance. The location chosen for the fort was a high bluff — Loftus Heights — overlooking the river, about seven miles south of Natchez. There "the situation" was thought to be healthful, not only because of climate but also because the troops would be quartered at a wholesome distance from the town's wickedness.

Natchez abounded in sins of various taints, although not to the extent of a few years later, after American control had become firmly established. The section of the city that lay "under the hill" — along the riverbank — was especially notorious; there every building not actually used for river commerce was said, in time, to have been given over to gambling, drinking, or prostitution. Murders were frequent.

Whereas the General acknowledged the need for some occasional proper diversion, the stern Governor Sargent saw only degradation in all of it. Early in his term he formed a very low opinion of the people who would tolerate the openness he saw in Natchez. He was, indeed, largely correct when he wrote the Secretary of State, "Diffused over our country are aliens of various characters and among them the most abandoned villains who have escaped from the chains and prisons of Spain." Not all of the violence in Natchez, however, could be attributed to aliens who had escaped from Spanish prisons. Some of it came from Sargent's fellow Anglo-Americans.

An example was a man named Condy, a frontiersman whose wild and roving disposition had not precluded his acquiring an attractive family: a wife and three children. The man's virulence was later recalled by a resident of early Natchez, in a contribution to an old book, *Mississippi, as a Province, Territory and State.*

Condy had begun to suspect his wife of carrying on an affair with a Spanish officer. Brooding over this, he became angrier and angrier until, one day, he cut his wife's throat with a razor, then killed all three children. He placed the bodies in a row on the ground, lay down beside them, and shot himself.

Professional criminals, too, infested the area, then and later, such as a band of brigands led by two men, Samuel Mason and Wiley Harp. From their rendezvous in cane-brakes near Walnut Hills they sallied forth to rob and kill, sometimes attacking the boats that plied the Mississippi. They kept an agent in Natchez to inform them of the arrival of tradesmen en route home by land from New Orleans after selling goods brought downriver. After the traders had left Natchez and begun their trip through the western wilderness up the lonely Natchez Trace to Nashville, fifteen or twenty days away, the bandits would lie in wait for them, steal their money, and either kill them or send them scurrying back to the comparative safety of Natchez.

Such lawlessness eventually resulted in Mason's death — in an ironic way, according to a tale passed down from early Mississippi days. From one unlucky traveler the gang took not only money, but also a circular containing a description of a reward offered for bringing in Mason, in any condition whatsoever. By chance, two members of the gang recently had been involved in an angry dispute with their leader, and the reward thus became doubly enticing to them: they could acquire some quick cash, and at the same time rid themselves of their antagonist. They caught Mason while he was alone, killed him, and cut off his head to take to nearby Greenville, Mississippi, where they intended to collect the money. There, according to the story, people who knew Mason had just finished identifying the grisly object as his head when the victimized traveler appeared and identified the two men as members of the band that had robbed him. They were tried and executed.

Even the Indians sometimes seemed to be more law-abiding. Rarely did tribesmen murder one another, and when they did, they did not often try to flee their punishment. Another tale out of Mississippi history illustrates this.

A Choctaw brave named Pi-in-tubbee quarreled with another warrior and in his passion killed him on the spot. He fled, but he knew he either had to die for his crime or forfeit the life of one of his kin, who would die in his place — and, worse, the entire family would be disgraced by the murderer's cowardice in not appearing for his punishment.

Pi-in-tubbee knew when the Choctaws were to gather for his execution, and where: on the forested crest of a hill overlooking a green valley. When the day arrived, however, the Indian was not there. His kin grew restive, then ashamed, until they saw him approaching from the valley below. He explained his tardiness and was preparing to die, the story went, when a missionary rode upon the scene, saw what was happening, and appealed to the Indians to pardon the condemned man. They refused.

Realizing the Indian was doomed, the missionary next considered Pi-in-tubbee's soul: he spoke knowingly to the unhappy savage of his many sins and depicted the horrors of hell with such force that the Indian showed increasing nervousness. Until then he had presumed that by surrendering his life to atone for his crime he would be rewarded by being permitted to pass on to the hunting grounds of his fathers. Now he became frightened.

Pi-in-tubbee's uncle noticed this and felt shame, then anger, that one of his blood should betray such weakness. He sank a tomahawk into Pi-in-tubbee's skull, and they buried him where he fell. Some women cried over his grave, it was said, but the warriors ended the day with a feast and a dance.

Although early Natchez reeked of violence and vulgarity, it had another side, too. The socially elite lived in mansions surrounded by handsomely landscaped grounds that effectively removed them from the unpleasantness nearby. Many of these people were haughty and totally self-sufficient, and they observed a strict social etiquette that seemed paradoxical on the frontier. A retinue of slaves served them, and these Negroes shared in the refinement. They were usually well treated: supplied with adequate clothing both summer and winter, given comfortable quarters, and sometimes even allowed to cultivate their own gardens and raise a few hogs and chickens. The monetary value of these slaves, of course, was largely responsible for their favorable treatment: a man was worth about five hundred dollars, a woman four hundred.

Nevertheless, the coarseness of Natchez outweighed its graces, particularly for the critical Governor Sargent. He despised the town and most of the people, and disapproved of the gaiety that prevailed on Sundays, when the populace indulged itself in pleasures ranging from picnics to gross carousing.

Recent ill health had left Sargent even more crotchety. "Natchez, from the perverseness of some of the people, and the [drunkenness] of the negroes and Indians on Sundays, has become a most abominable place," he wrote in a letter, and he asked General Wilkinson for army help in maintaining order in the town. Wilkinson, whose own fondness for merrymaking was well known, complied diplomatically, but he might have agreed privately with a Natchez citizen who once wrote to a friend, "It is impossible that a man so frigid and sour [as Sargent] can give satisfaction to a free people."

While Wilkinson was humoring Sargent and charming Ellicott, his onetime protégé Philip Nolan was away in Texas after more wild horses, and perhaps engaging in some less obvious activity: he had taken with him the field glasses and timepiece given him by Andrew Ellicott, and a sextant donated by the Spaniard Gayoso. These instruments would be used in making maps.

Nolan's current expedition had been planned in 1797. On April 24 of that year Nolan had written Wilkinson:

> ... I have got such a passport, that I apprehend neither risk nor detention; I have instruments to enable me to make, a more correct map than the one you saw; Ellicott assisted me in acquiring a more perfect knowledge of astronomy and glasses; and Gayoso himself has made me a present of a portable sextant. My time piece is good. I shall pay every attention, and take an assistant with me, who is a tolerable mathematician....

Nolan's passport had not been issued to him, however, until almost two months after the date of this letter. On June 17 Carondelet had given him written approval "to supply this province with horses from the Province of Texas." The Louisiana governor also had written to Governor Muñoz at San Antonio.

> The good qualities and the loyalty displayed by Philip Nolan, the bearer of this letter, who is known in that province, have moved me to recommend him to you that you may ex-

tend your protection to him. It is his purpose to secure more horses for this province, where, on account of the increase in population, the cold, and the floods, there is a scarcity.

This young man will not deviate from a strict obedience to our laws, nor from the particular orders that you may give him. The favor you show must redound to your benefit.

Other documents of this period pose a mystery as to Nolan's loyalty and intentions. The solution died with him more than a century and a half ago; only guesses are possible now. Some existing documents provide a basis for conjecture:

In March, around the time Gayoso had written Nolan his inquiry, "What political interest do you embrace?" Nolan had offered the Natchez official an even split of the profits to be made during his coming expedition, possibly because he had heard that Gayoso was due to move into a more influential position as successor to Carondelet, the governor of Louisiana. Gayoso had replied with a cordial letter in which he stated, without putting on paper an acceptance, "I assure you, my friend, that for a long time I have desired the opportunity of expressing to you the sincere affection I feel for you. No one better knows your worth; also no one more than I, interests himself more in the advancement of your fortune. . . . The plan which you have communicated to me, and of which I approve, is the one most suitable for you. . . . I shall content myself with the recommendation to you that you look well to those with whom you form connections that might work injury to the most useful and the easiest way of executing your plans in order to assure their good success and avoid contingencies."

Later Nolan obtained recommendations in his behalf from New Orleans priests to their counterparts in Texas, and in

May he reported this fact to Gayoso, who replied, ". . . Am very glad of the additional good prospect that offers for your future campaign as I do not doubt but the new recommendations will be productive of the best effects."

Some other persons claimed they heard a different tune from Nolan. One of them was Samuel Moore, a New Orleans citizen who was to recall, years later, these months in Nolan's career. "On the subject of what was confided to me, by Philip Nolan . . . , this gentleman, when last in this city, in the month of May, or June, 1797, after offering me a concern with him, in the privilege he had obtained . . . from the Baron de Carondelet, to trade and bring out horses from the province of Texas, did tell me, 'that he had obtained proper passports and strong recommendations from some of the priests here, to those of that country.' "

I asked him how he had made out to procure those advantages [Moore continued]. He said "through General Wilkinson's recommendation to the Governor: that the Baron expected him to make discoveries, and give him plans and information of the country he should explore; but," said Nolan, "I shall take good care to give him no information, unless such may be calculated to mislead him. Whatever discoveries I can make shall be carefully preserved for General Wilkinson, for the benefit of our government. As to myself" said Nolan, "I have already rendered myself popular among those *Ouatchinangoes*, and I shall study to render myself more so. I look forward to the conquest of Mexico by the United States; and I expect my patron and friend, the General, will, in such an event, give me a conspicuous command"; he added, "that he would endeavor to penetrate towards the sea-shore of that country and discover, where ports might be found; that unless for the danger of the Osage Indians, he could, by a short route, take his horses to Kentucky, by way of the Illinois country."

Like Nolan, Gayoso proved capable of double-dealing: for some reason he became bitter toward Nolan and, in time, would seek his undoing. Perhaps his animosity came partly as a reaction against Americans generally. By June 1797, Gayoso and Ellicott had argued with such force that their outwardly cordial relationship had abruptly disintegrated. Furthermore, there had existed the threat of war, and Wilkinson had been trumpeting his patriotism and military prowess for his fellow Americans to see. These developments might have caused Gayoso to become more suspicious of Nolan by simple association, or perhaps he had intercepted some incriminating correspondence or overheard talk that had convinced him of Nolan's unreliability. Whatever the reason, Gayoso seems to have lost faith in the man. At least Nolan said so, in a letter to Wilkinson written from Natchez July 21:

> Gayoso is a vile man, and my implacable enemy; yet, he treats me with attention. During the commotions here, he wrote to the Baron, requesting, that he would not permit me to leave Orleans — 'he will take an active part against us, he is popular, and enterprising; secure him.' — Under the same cover, he subscribed himself my friend; and, but a few days before, made me a present of a sextant. The Baron knows him, and has done all in his power, to secure me from his vengeance. I have, however, my fears; and I may yet be obliged to shoot the monster with a poisoned arrow.

Eleven days after Nolan wrote this letter, Carondelet was replaced by none other than Gayoso as governor at New Orleans, and Nolan's fortunes then began a slow but steady decline. Nevertheless, during the latter part of July 1797, he left on his latest expedition into Texas, after waiting until the war threat had eased. With him were two Americans, four Spaniards, and two slaves. For trading he took seven thousand dollars' worth of merchandise and "twelve good rifles." All the goods were to be used in exchange for wild horses, to be sold for profits of which one-third was to go to one of the Americans, who had invested some two thousand dollars in the enterprise.

At Nacogdoches Nolan visited the Leals and renewed his liaison with Gertrudis, then went on to San Antonio, where he presented his passport to Governor Muñoz during the first days of October 1797. At this point Nolan, whose impetuousness quickly became obvious to acquaintances, grew too cocksure for his own good. He falsely claimed to have a "commission" for procuring horses for the Louisiana regiment, and indicated he had received approval from Carondelet of his seeking them in Nuevo Santander, specifically in an area between the Nueces and Río Grande rivers where the mustangs abounded.

Muñoz, who was as taken by Nolan's engaging personality as Carondelet, forwarded the passport to Pedro de Nava, commanding general of the interior provinces whose headquarters were at Chihuahua, along with a letter in which he declared that Nolan possessed a recommendation from Carondelet to the governor of Nuevo Santander in behalf of Nolan's entry into that province.

Adding a Wilkinsonian touch, Nolan sent along a gift to Nava: a new gun, with instructions on its use. He offered to supply as many of the weapons as Nava might want, at a moderate cost. Further, he offered to map the country under Nava's command, after he had obtained his wild horses.

The gift, along with Muñoz' and Nolan's letters, brought the favorable response Nolan had sought: Nava instructed

Muñoz to do whatever he could to help Nolan get his horses. Nava also wrote Nolan directly, telling him about these instructions. He added, however, that the request to enter Nuevo Santander would have to go to the governor of that province for approval. As for the map, Nava declared he would be glad to see one.

Now Nolan began to pull wires that, in the end, only served to trip him up. The priests' recommendations he sent to a friend of theirs, Francisco Rendón, former intendant at New Orleans who currently held a similar post at Zacatecas, along with a plea that Rendón speak for him to Commanding General Nava and to the governor of Nuevo Santander. Nolan described the "commission" he claimed to have and the recommendation for his admittance to Nuevo Santander he said he had obtained from Carondelet. He added that he had unfortunately lost this letter.

At Zacatecas, Rendón read Nolan's plea and was not immediately persuaded by the slick wording, as had been many of Nolan's other Spanish contacts. Instead, Rendón addressed a query to Carondelet, who was by that time in Ecuador, for verification of Nolan's claims. After some time Carondelet answered that Nolan had no "commission" from him to get the horses, and that he, Carondelet, had not written a letter to the governor of Nuevo Santander in Nolan's behalf. Carondelet said, however, that he trusted Nolan and that he had indeed given him a passport and a letter to the governor of Texas, where Nolan had originally said he expected to procure the horses. Rendón sent Carondelet's reply to the Viceroy, the Marquis de Branciforte, for advice.

Unfortunately for Nolan, Gayoso had reached the Viceroy's ear before Rendón. Soon after Gayoso assumed the governorship of Louisiana he wrote the Viceroy that a group of Americans planned to enter Texas to win the support of the Indians and to brew a revolution. Gayoso suggested to the Viceroy that he order the arrest of any foreigner entering the province, and he especially advised a careful watch be kept on Nolan.

The Viceroy sent Gayoso's letter to Nava, who commenced trying to explain Nolan's presence in the provinces, with obvious dismay. Nava touched on the Royal Order of 1780 allowing importation of horses to Louisiana, said he knew nothing derogatory about Nolan, but promised to arrest the man if this proved necessary for the good of the province.

There the matter rested for a while — until Branciforte was succeeded as viceroy in 1798 by Miguel José de Azanza, who became curious about Nolan's activities soon after assuming his duties. Azanza wrote Carondelet, inquiring anew about the passport. Carondelet replied with much the same information he had given Rendón, and Azanza instructed Nava to order Nolan out of Texas. Nava replied that Nolan already had left — in July of 1798 — and the Viceroy felt relieved.

His comfortable feeling was to be shattered.

Nolan had not left Texas after all, although Nava did not know it. Breakdowns in communications were frequent in the Spanish New World; long distances separated various Spanish officials. Travel was slow and information sometimes unreliable.

Nava learned of Nolan's continued presence quite by accident — in a 1799 letter from Texas Governor Muñoz, who casually reported punishing a band of Indians for stealing Nolan's horses. Astounded, Nava replied that he had understood Nolan returned to New Orleans during the preceding year.

Nava's suspicions now became thoroughly aroused, and he asked Muñoz for an evaluation of Nolan. The governor, still Nolan's friend, declared him to be a trustworthy man, one who could be counted on to support Spain, and said that it would be unwise to alienate this "enterprising young man of good education; who had acquired more than an ordinary knowledge about the country of both provinces, not only because of his long residence in them, but because of his industrious nature, his natural comprehension, and his knowledge of geography." As for Nolan's extended visit in Spanish territory, Muñoz wrote, he saw nothing to worry about. Nolan had required much time, the governor emphasized, for his work: building corrals and fences, acquiring a total of more than twelve hundred horses, and making that trip to Nuevo Santander.

Nava must have been furious when he read this news — that Nolan had visited Nuevo Santander without approval — but no doubt his mood changed to anxiety when he began to draft his report to the Viceroy. Worse, sometime after he received the bewildering intelligence from Muñoz, a letter arrived from Gayoso declaring that Nolan was a dangerous man, a hypocrite who was loud in his avowal of Catholicism when he was among Spaniards but who scorned the religion when among Americans. Furthermore, Gayoso said, Nolan probably was mapping the country for General Wilkinson, who had plans of conquering it. Six weeks after Gayoso wrote this letter he was stricken with an illness and died, but his passing came too late to save Nolan from being a much-wanted man.

Muñoz, too, died about this time — little more than one month after his letter to Nava had been written. Perhaps his death was both timely and fortunate for him, since deliberate laxity on his part allowed Nolan to get out of Texas even after Muñoz had promised, finally, to tell Nolan about his banishment from the province. Had Muñoz been energetic, he could have dispatched troops to intercept Nolan on Spanish soil. Instead, the governor dawdled and Nolan rode out from within the jaws of Spanish vengeance without realizing that his presumptuous actions had alerted so many important people in so many places. By November 1799, he had concluded what proved to be a profitable, if dangerous, expedition.

In the United States he heard of his close call and dispatched a gift of Irish linen to Gertrudis in Nacogdoches for presentation to the commandant, to "make all things right," and sent a double-barreled shotgun to a Franciscan friend there, Father José Manuel Gaetán.

Upon his return, Nolan also read a long letter addressed to him from the Vice President of the United States; it had arrived during his absence. The communication had been delivered to Daniel Clark, Jr., of New Orleans, along with all other mail received in his absence, in compliance with instructions Nolan had left prior to his departure.

Philadelphia June 24. 1798

Sir

It was some time since I have understood that there are large herds of horses in a wild state in the country West of the Mississippi and have been desirous of obtaining details of their history in that state. Mr. . . . Brown, Senator from Kentucky, informs me it would be in your power to give interesting information on this subject, and encourages me to ask it. the circumstances of the old-world have, beyond the records of history, been such as admitted not that animal to exist in a state of nature. the condition of America is rapidly advancing to the same. the present then is probably the only moment in the age of the world and the herds above mentioned the only subjects, of which we can avail ourselves to obtain what has never yet been recorded and never can be again in all probability. I will add that your information is the sole reliance, as far as I can at present see, for obtaining this desideratum you will render to natural history a very acceptable service therefore, if you will enable our Philosophical-society to add so interesting a chapter to the history of the animal. I need not specify to you the particular facts asked for, as your knowledge of the animal in his domesticated, as well as his wild state, will naturally have led your attention to those particulars in the manners, habits, & laws of his existence, which are peculiar to his wild state. I wish you not to be anxious about the form of your information. the exactness of the substance alone is material: and if, after giving in a first letter all the facts you at present possess, you could be so good, on subsequent occasions, as to furnish such others in addition as you may acquire from time to time, your communication will always be thankfully received. If addressed to me at Monticello & put into any post office of Kentucky or Tenissee, they will reach me speedily & safely, and will be considered as obligations on Sir

Your most obedt. &
humble servt
TH: JEFFERSON

Clark already had acknowledged receipt of the letter to Jefferson, explaining Nolan's absence and commenting that he had been given "directions from [Nolan] to peruse all Letters addressed to him previous to their being forwarded that in case of accident, no expression contained in them should awaken the jealousy of the auspicious people among whom he has by coincidence of fortunate circumstances introduced himself. . . . I must suggest to you the necessity of keeping to yourself for the present all the information that may be forwarded to you as the slightest Hint would point out the Channel from whence it flowed and might probably be attended with the most fatal consequences to a man, who will at all times have it in his Power to render important services to the U.S., and whom Nature seems to have formed for Enterprizes of which the rest of Mankind are incapable."

Clark added a warning, ". . . it will require all the good Opinion you may have been led to entertain of his veracity not to have your Belief staggered with the accounts you will receive of the numbers, & habits of the Horses of that Country and the people who live in that Neighborhood whose Customs & ideas are as different from ours as those of the Hordes of Grand Tartary."

Clark happened to be visiting at a commodious Natchez estate, "the Forest," owned by William Dunbar, when Nolan arrived from his expedition. So, after his return to his home in New Orleans, Clark again wrote Jefferson, on November 12:

Whilst at [Dunbar's] House we had the satisfaction of seeing Mr. Phillip Nolan arrive from New Mexico [meaning Texas], he has brought with him 1000 head of Horses and by a singular favor of Providence has escaped the snares which were laid for him — Gayoso the late Governor of the Province of Louisiana, a few months before his Death wrote to the Governor of Texas . . . to arrest Nolan on his return as a Person who from the Knowledge he had acquired of the interior parts of New Mexico, might one day be of injury to the Spanish Monarchy, the thing would have been effected according to his Wish & Nolan might probably have been confined for life on mere suspicion. . . .

... The certainty that the blind yet suspicious people would never believe that he could correspond with a Person in your high Station on any subject unconnected with Politics induced me to request you would give nothing to the World which could be traced to him, for any Communication, how innocent so ever in itself would be suspected & in case of delivery would have been fatal — He has no longer anything to fear on this Head and he proposes shortly forwarding you the information you require.

Clark's letter indicated that he believed Nolan was not planning to return to Texas: "He has no longer anything to fear on this Head."

Nolan himself said as much. In a letter dated November 20, 1799, he wrote a man he had employed as his agent in Nacogdoches, John Cook, to say that he would not try to return to Texas because of Gayoso's "treachery." Nolan told Cook to brand some horses left behind with Gertrudis' mark, and to consult Nolan's Franciscan friend, Father Gaetán, if there were problems.

Further indication that Nolan intended to settle down came with his acquisition of a bride. His charms had fallen heavily on Frances Lintot, a fetching, though quiet, young lady who was the daughter of a widely known Natchez planter. His masculine attraction, characterized by his exciting stories of adventure in Texas, was strong enough to pull the girl away from her parents — especially from her father, who did not approve of Nolan, a "common horse trader," he said, of no means and no family.

Lintot tried to break up the romance, but without success. His daughter continued to see Nolan, slipping out of the house to do it, and when it became apparent to Lintot that he could either give his approval to the marriage or see Fanny elope, he surrendered. The wedding, in the Lintot home six days before Christmas of 1799, was a notable social event in Natchez. A justice of the peace joined the couple "in Holy State of Matrimony agreeably to the laws of this Territory." The holy state lasted only a short time, however, before Nolan caught the Texas fever again. For whatever reason, he grew eager to travel westward once more: westward to adventure and fortune and whatever else it was that Nolan was looking for there — westward, perhaps, to Gertrudis, to whom Nolan continued to write affectionate letters: "My Very esteemed and Beloved Gertrudis . . . When I have a dollar I will give the half to thee . . . In thee I have much confidence . . . Farewell my dear Gertrudis."

In the middle of 1800 Nolan journeyed to Philadelphia, to visit Thomas Jefferson. Oddly, he seems also to have visited representatives of Great Britain while he was in the East. Britain displayed an avid interest in affairs in the West and would have been pleased by the formation of a new republic there; such a development would have weakened both Spain and the United States, to Britain's benefit.

Nolan carried to Jefferson an introduction from his former patron and Jefferson's close friend, General Wilkinson, written at Fort Adams and dated May 22, 1800:

> In the Bearer of this Letter — Mr. P. Nolan, you will behold the Mexican traveller, a specimen of whose discoveries, I had the Honor to submit to you in the Winter 1797, Mr. N—s subsequent excursions have been more extensive, & his observations more accurate, He feels pride in offering Himself to your investigation, and I am persuaded you will find pleasure, in his details of a Country, the Soil, clime, population, improvements & productions of which are so little known to us.

An acquaintance of many Years, from his Early Youth, authorizes me to vouch for Mr. N—s high sense of probity — dare I Sir, I would recommend Him to your kindness & acknowledge myself obliged by any Courtesy you may offer to Him —

Jefferson conferred with Nolan for hours, although government officials were engaged in a hectic move from Philadelphia to the new capital at Washington, D.C. Some persons have speculated that the two discussed more momentous subjects than the habits of wild horses in the West, and some even said that Nolan had not really intended to return to Texas until Jefferson convinced him that he should, to learn more about the country for an eventual United States take-over.

The evidence against such intrigue, however, is strong. The Vice President had a genuine interest in many subjects, particularly those relating to the natural sciences. Furthermore, he was president of the American Philosophical Society, which published studies in many fields. Jefferson had every reason to be interested in nothing more than the habits of wild horses west of the Mississippi, and this probably was true. If Nolan's return to Texas was for ulterior purposes, the motivation probably came from someone else besides Jefferson.

The change in the governorship at New Orleans seemed fortunate for Nolan — his enemy Gayoso was gone — until the new governor, Casa Calvo, showed himself to be as distrustful of Americans as his predecessor. Nevertheless, after returning from Philadelphia Nolan applied to Casa Calvo for a passport "to run the pasture lands to the north" — meaning to the north of the settlements at Nacogdoches and San Antonio. The governor promptly refused permission. Probably he had received word of Nolan's visit to the seat of United States government, which would have doubled the concern he already felt.

Nolan's way was being blocked also in Texas. The commanding general of the interior provinces, Pedro de Nava, had become convinced, finally, that Nolan was a dangerous man, and on August 8, 1800, he ordered the new Texas governor, Elguezábal, to arrest the intruder "with the greatest secrecy" if he again appeared in the province. "You will have an inventory made of his property," Nava said, "which you will forward to me with the papers found on his person." Should Nolan be apprehended, Nava wanted Elguezábal to get answers to some vital questions. Where had Nolan been for the past few years? What was his native country? What were his residence, occupation, religion, citizenship? Had he sold any of his captured horses in the United States? Was he working for General Wilkinson?

Nava indicated that he believed he already knew most of the answers. In the same letter he wrote, "I have positive information that Philip Nolan is an Anglo American, and his conduct gives me good cause to suspect that his visit to your province had other objects in view than those stated in his passport, and avowed by him. . . . There are sufficient grounds to believe that he is instructed to report his discoveries in [the United States]."

Nava added the information Gayoso had provided about Nolan's pretensions of accepting Catholicism, then said, ". . . Great caution should be used in questioning, and trying to get the truth out of that shrewd man who will, of course, endeavor to give such coloring to his designs as to remove suspicion." Nolan's companions, if captured, were to be questioned separately. "Should any discrepancy be observed between their and Nolan's declarations, they should be confronted."

Nolan did not know of Nava's order, of course, but he was clearly aware of the Spanish opposition to his future expeditions. Nevertheless, in Natchez he began planning another journey into Spanish territory despite Casa Calvo's refusal of a passport.

Just across the river from Natchez, the commandant of the Spanish post at Concordia, José Vidal, heard the talk of Nolan's plans with growing alarm. An agent in Natchez had been keeping Vidal informed of Nolan's movements and of the expedition plans even as Nolan made them. After Nolan's serious intent had become clear, Vidal dispatched a warning to Governor Juan Bautista Elguezábal at San Antonio that "Philip Nolan, a native of Ireland and a citizen of the United States," planned to travel without permission into the province of Texas "with 30 or 40 Americans" armed with rifles, to an area north of San Antonio known as Los Llanos ("The Plains"). Vidal asserted that his information indicated Nolan was determined to go through with his plans at any cost, and was prepared to fight if necessary. Vidal continued, in words that reflected the worry of all Spanish officialdom:

> The insult intended by that man Nolan to his Majesty's territory might have fatal consequences if not checked. Should he succeed, others would follow his example, and embark in like expeditions; Americans would, by degrees, penetrate these precious possessions, which it is so important to conceal from the ambition of the United States.

Vidal also informed Casa Calvo at New Orleans that Nolan "has in his service men who with their guns can enter and defend themselves against any force." To Lieutenant Miguel de Músquiz, commandant at Nacogdoches, Vidal wrote "under seal of secrecy" a letter warning that Nolan had many friends in Natchez, Nacogdoches, and San Antonio: "It will, therefore, be of great importance not to acquaint anyone, except perhaps a few officers, with the measures you deem advisable to take. Nolan is active, enterprising and resolute, and better acquainted with the country than the natives themselves. Cook and some other men . . . are also dangerous characters; therefore I request you not to allow anyone to discover the channel through which you have obtained information, as an indiscretion might endanger my life, and deprive me of the power of keeping you informed. . . ." Vidal continued, in a dilatory tone typically Spanish, "I am satisfied that that man can be captured on his return, if he succeeds in slipping through your Province."

While Nolan continued to make his plans, Vidal tried to restrain him with legal maneuvering. Early in October he complained to Governor Sargent about Nolan. A week later he wrote out a formal accusation and sent it to Sargent, declaring Nolan's intentions — as Vidal had heard them — to be clearly in defiance of "the Laws of the Kingdom," a danger to international peace, and a threat, in fact, to Nolan himself.

Sargent summoned Nolan before the Supreme Court of the Mississippi Territory. There Vidal also appeared, to ask that the court prohibit Nolan from entering Spanish territory.

Before the court Nolan declared that he was indeed preparing to return to Texas, but that he had Spanish authority to do so. As verification he produced the old letter from Pedro de Nava, written in 1798, saying that Nava would be glad to see a map of the interior provinces and that Governor

Muñoz had been instructed to help him as much as possible in gathering the horses.

Vidal argued that the letter was no longer valid, that Nolan himself knew very well now that he had been a fugitive when he left Texas the last time, and that Nolan could not honestly expect to be permitted to return to that province. If he went anyway, Vidal declared, Spain could only consider his intentions as hostile, as strongly armed as he would be.

Nolan, with fatal self-assurance, replied that the weapons he and his men planned to take were not meant to be used aggressively, but only in defense — against thieves and Indians — and in procuring game.

The court decided Vidal had not presented sufficient evidence to permit any interference with Nolan's plans. ". . . It is beyond our power and contrary to the Constitution of the United States," Vidal reported the chief justice as saying, "to prevent . . . citizens from leaving their territory when it cannot be proved with evidence that their intentions are hostile."

Vidal continued to voice his disagreement. The chief justice tried to placate him by declaring that if Nolan committed crimes on Spanish territory he could expect to stand trial in Spanish courts. The chief justice promised that if Nolan should flee as a fugitive to the United States he would be returned to face appropriate royal prosecution.

So Nolan, the intrepid — foolhardy, it seemed — Irishman concluded his plans to depart. His wife Fanny was pregnant, and surely she could not have been happy about being left in that condition with her parents, whom she had more or less forsaken for the dashing adventurer only a few months earlier. Nolan, however, was not a man to let this matter interfere with ambition.

Exactly why he returned to Texas against such strong Spanish opposition never became clear. His plan at this time — according to information contained in an expedition contract found later, with other items, in a trunk — was to return to Natchez in three months. This certainly would not have been long enough to give him time to engage in much deviltry against Spain, especially if he actually expected to bring back horses.

Various people, including Spaniards, guessed afterward that Nolan went west to map the country for conquest; to look for gold and silver; to plunder; to stir up the Indians for a rebellion; to find true happiness with Gertrudis — although he remarked to an acquaintance that he did not expect, or desire, to see her; or simply to get his wild horses.

One attraction above all others, however, probably drew Nolan westward for his perilous quest: the exhilaration of riding boldly into still-unknown lands, of living free from the encumbrances which even a frontier society imposed and in rhythm only with nature, and of seeing things that no other white man had seen — like the "uncommon Animal . . . seen by the Natives in a considerable lake in a sequestered situation in New Mexico [meaning Texas]."

Nolan had not actually seen the animal, but one can imagine his desire to do so. He told William Dunbar, a Natchez man of enlightenment, about the phenomenon, and Dunbar reported the conversation in a letter to Thomas Jefferson.

It is compared when somewhat elevated in the water, to the upper part of the body of a Spaniard with his broad brimmed hat, & . . . it is often hear'd to breathe or blow heavily. The Indians who are often Superstitious express a dislike or abhorrence of the place, seldom going near it, and assert that

the departed Spirits of the first Spaniards who conquered their
Country dwell in the lake. Mr. Nolan informed me that he
was once very near that lake, but knew nothing of it untill
some time after, when he was told the above circumstances.
Whether we are to suppose this a fable invented by the Indians — or that there really exists an Animal, perhaps the
hippopotamus or a nondescript, will remain the discovery of
a future time.

The creature probably was a manatee, or sea cow, and the
"lake" probably was a lagoon along the Gulf of Mexico. In
Nolan's day manatees were plentiful in that region, and
those strange mammals could easily have fit the old Indian
description. Possibly a manatee originally contributed to the
mermaid legend, because of its occasional human appearance:
when feeding, it holds its body in a vertical stance, head and
shoulders above water, and sweeps food into its mouth with
rapid movements of its flippers. From a distance these flippers might have resembled the brim of a hat.

Now Nolan was bound again for this strange land, realizing
that the "Spaniard with his broad brimmed hat" could be
very much alive and not at all a departed spirit in some remote
lake. Obviously, he was not deterred by this chilling prospect.

Nolan dispatched a messenger to the agent Cook in Nacogdoches with this letter:

Natchez Oct. 21, 1800
Dear Cook: — It seems that they are all busying themselves
to catch some information about the trip I intend to make to
the West. I wanted to go to the Rio Grande, leaving Nacogdoches somewhat to the North; but owing to the reports already made on my intentions, I shall take my course along
the coast, to avoid the troops of Nacogdoches who will certainly go out to look for me.

As you value my friendship keep the secret.

I take with me a large stock of goods, but they all think I am going to run mustangs. I expect to be back in January.

I know from certain information, that if you do not, as soon as you receive this letter, gather up all your stock of cattle and mine, and drive them off, we shall lose the whole of them. Mind my advice, dear friend, and do not lose one moment to leave the place. I have heard that Vidal has some information about my intentions, and did forward it to Nacogdoches. But never fear; I have good men with me, and they will never catch us.

I am so well acquainted with the coast from Opelousas to the Rio Grande, that they will never be able to overtake and attack us. I have everything well arranged at Revilla that I shall not be detained two days in that place.

As soon as you have read this letter, burn it.

PHILIP NOLAN

Some sentences in Nolan's letter pose a mystery not explained to this day: ". . . they all think I am going to run mustangs"; "I have everything well arranged at Revilla. . . ." If Nolan was not going to run mustangs, and if he really expected to return by January — within three months — what was his actual intention?

The last sentence, however, left no room for doubt. Nolan considered the letter fatally incriminating: ". . . burn it."

Cook had no chance to burn the letter, or even to read it. Vidal's espionage network had forewarned that Nolan's messenger would be en route to Nacogdoches with a letter to Cook, and the man was apprehended by the Spaniards at Rapides, in the province of Louisiana. Eagerly his captors read the letter, perhaps with perplexity and surely with alarm, and saved it — for posterity, as it happened.

8. INTO FORBIDDEN LANDS

PHILIP NOLAN was to commence his forbidden journey into
Texas with twenty-seven men, including a dauntless seventeen-year-old son of the American frontier, Peter Ellis Bean.

No description exists of Bean's physical appearance at this
age. One can only imagine him as a plain-faced lad, probably of medium height, whose light brown hair reflected his
Scotch-Irish ancestry. His complexion would have been ruddy
from exposure to the weather, and his body would have been
wiry and hard from helping his father with heavy work on
their farm in the wild country around Bean Station, on the
Holston River, in what is now Grainger County in East Tennessee. He came from a line of Indian-fighters; and from his

relatives he learned about guns and powder. This was knowledge that would later prove very beneficial.

Bean's psychology is more easily deduced. His wanderlust epitomized the times. On the American frontier, where plenty of land was available farther on, families broke up early and without tears. In those days a possible inheritance meant nothing to most young people; frequently the only legacy would have been more hard work. Young members of the family sought their fortune the same way their fathers had: by moving to the lush valley on the far side of the mountain, or to some other place. They had been reared to work, to think for themselves, to watch out for their scalps in perilous surroundings.

Bean showed himself to be such a youth, in the only detailed account of his life he left behind: his *Memoir*, written around 1816 and included in the first volume of Henderson King Yoakum's two-volume *History of Texas*, originally published in 1855. Yoakum edited the *Memoir*, but presumably did not tamper with the facts: in a note preceding the text he said, "In publishing this memoir, it is proper to state that Colonel Bean was but poorly educated. . . . Hence it has become necessary to correct his manuscript, and to rewrite it. In doing this, great care has been taken to preserve, as far as possible, his style and language."

In the *Memoir* Bean comes through as a strong-willed youth eager to hack out his own path through the wilderness, and as a boy not likely to crawl back home once he had walked out. Family meant little to him: he mentioned his relatives on only the first two pages of the fifty-page autobiography, and mentioned them briefly and unemotionally at that.

"I was born in the state of Tennessee, in the year 1783," he wrote. "I had a common education given me, and such as a frontier country could afford." Virtually nothing else is known of Bean's youth, except that according to Spanish records of a later date his family religion as stated by him was Anabaptist.

At the age of seventeen years [Bean wrote], I had a great desire to travel, and see other parts of the world. To see some foreign country was all my desire. My father said I was too young, and would not consent. But as the town of Natchez had fallen to the United States, and was a good market for the produce of Tennessee, he consented that I might bring to that country [down the Holston, Tennessee, Ohio, and Mississippi rivers] a boat-load of whiskey and flour; all of which being made ready in a few days, I started in company with a young man from the same place, by the name of John Word, who had some lading with me. About three hundred miles below Knoxville, in a place called the Muscle-shoals, I broke my boat in pieces on a rock, and lost all my cargo. I only saved a small trunk of clothes. My companion concluded then that he would return; but I would not, for I wished to see that country.

Bean had only five dollars to see him southward down the circuitous river route: along the course of the winding Tennessee to the Ohio and thence to the Mississippi into Natchez. In addition to the money, however, he had youthful exuberance, optimism, and curiosity — assets that could not be calculated in his meager finances, though they represented wealth nevertheless. Furthermore, he knew he had relatives in the town downriver, and from them he probably hoped to borrow money.

Soon after his wreck he found passage on a family boat bound for Natchez. Climbing aboard with the people and their few possessions, he joined the stream of emigrants drifting westward with the current.

Surprisingly, he was expected at Natchez. After landing he was walking down a sandy beach at the river's edge when a small boy approached him to inquire if the boat on which he had arrived was from Tennessee.

"I told him it was," Bean wrote in his *Memoir*. "He then asked me if there was any man on board by the name of Bean. I told him that was my name. He said his mistress had told him that if there was any one on the boat of that name, he must come to the house with him."

Predictably, Bean, surely puzzled by this development, refused to go with the boy, who left to carry the news home. For the next half hour Bean continued his stroll, taking in the sights, smells, and sounds of this strange new place. Then he was sought out by the boy's mother, who proved to be Bean's aunt, and her daughter. He accepted an invitation to stay with them.

He promptly became unhappy; perhaps the family consisted entirely of the aunt, her daughters, and some small boys — an overwhelmingly unappealing group for a seventeen-year-old lad whose immediate purpose was to see the world. After one night Bean wrote a newly located uncle, twelve miles distant, a plea to send for him, and the uncle dispatched a man with a horse and saddle. Bean moved to his uncle's house, where the surroundings proved more congenial. Still, life was not all pleasant: after two weeks Bean fell sick, and for a month he lay seriously ill. Then his health began to return.

In his *Memoir* he wrote:

> In this time I got acquainted with a man by the name of Nolan, that had been for some years before trading with the Spaniards in San Antonio. He told me that he was going to

make another voyage to that country in October, and entreated me to go along with him. I readily agreed to go, and stated it to my uncle. But he would not hear of it, and said that I should not go. A few days afterward my uncle and aunt were absent from home, and Nolan came by, with some young men, then on his voyage. I immediately saddled my horse and started, to make a voyage for three months; and when my relations came home in the evening, I was gone. . . .

Possibly Bean never saw his uncle or aunt again: his "voyage" was to last much longer than three months. He departed, however, with spirits high and with no concern about the outcome of his adventure. In his *Memoir* he inserted a footnote: "Before we left Natchez, Governor Sargent and Judge Bruin [of the Supreme Court] had called a court on the complaint of the Spanish consul Vidal; but, finding our passport, that we had from the commandant-general, Don Pedro de Nava, to be good, it was agreed by the court that Nolan should go. . . ."

Nolan had negotiated contracts with Bean and all the other expedition members, with the probable exception of two slaves. Each man was to take his own horses and weapons, help build corrals and pens, and help in catching wild horses. Nolan would provide food and ammunition and a predetermined number of the horses taken — the figure varying from man to man according to his estimated worth — plus a stipulated sum of money for each day the expedition lasted beyond three months. David Fero, a former United States Army lieutenant, was to be second-in-command and would be rewarded with seven horses, and a dollar for every day his employment lasted beyond the three-month period. Less compensation was to go to seven men who seemed to be risking more than anyone else: they were citizens of New Spain.

The date probably was October 30, 1800, when Nolan and his men left Natchez, riding northward — not southward for the coast, as the captured letter to Cook had indicated. Perhaps Nolan had heard of its loss, or maybe he had written it to mislead the Spaniards. Whatever the case, Nolan indeed had confused them at least temporarily: Vidal had written the commandant at Nacogdoches, Lieutenant Músquiz, on October 20 that Nolan planned to travel southward along the Gulf Coast.

The two slaves, mounted, led pack horses carrying bundles of goods and equipment: tools, blankets, cloth of bright colors for trading with the Indians, branding irons, and iron hobbles. A chill in the morning air hinted of the arrival of autumn, but this soon gave way to summer warmth as the sun arced higher in a humid sky. Keeping to the lofty east bank of the river, Nolan's men traveled along a line of eroded, yellow-brown bluffs overlooking the silently flowing Mississippi and, beyond the river, a tangled wilderness that rolled westward toward the horizon — a pastel sargasso sea that dared voyagers to enter. This land belonged to Spain.

Apparently most of the men presumed, as had Bean, that their leader owned a valid passport, but of course Nolan knew this was not true. Nevertheless, on November 1 he ushered his men across the Mississippi at the place then called Walnut Hills — now Vicksburg — near where the Spaniards had maintained their old fort of Nogales. Probably Nolan's men built rafts for the crossing, unless they had access to more substantial boats. They would have loaded the animals and other possessions thereon and paddled swiftly for the low-lying shore on the other side.

From the Spanish bank they set out almost due west, through a gloomy, swampy wasteland inhabited only by alligators and other wildlife, towards the Ouachita River sixty or seventy miles distant. They would cross it somewhere near the present site of Monroe, Louisiana.

If the men felt secure through ignorance of the nonexistent passport, Nolan's assuredness came from a deeper source. Every man in his party was well equipped to defend himself — with shotguns, carbines, pistols. Nolan himself carried a double-barreled shotgun, two pistols, and a carbine; and people later said they had heard him boast that his men could outfight any force the Spaniards might throw against him.

Now, it seemed, he would have a chance to prove his statement. His movements had continued to attract the surveillance of José Vidal, from his fort on the opposite bank of the river from Natchez, and Vidal had alerted Spanish posts along the frontier about Nolan's departure. Although every Spanish official from the Viceroy to the lowliest subaltern awaited with anticipation word of Nolan's capture, most of them seemed content to let the other man handle the disagreeable task of taking him. Perhaps never before had a force of twenty-eight men inspired such fear in a major power.

The vacillation began as Nolan neared the Ouachita River on November 6, when a mounted force of nineteen Spanish militiamen dispatched from Fort Ouachita intercepted his expedition, but decided not to risk a fight. "We asked them their business," Bean wrote later in his *Memoir*. "They told us they were in pursuit of some Choctaw Indians, that had stolen some horses. This was false, for they were hunting our party, though they were afraid to own it."

The Spaniards, including an armed priest, filed on into the

woods after their "Choctaws," returned shortly, then can-
tered off in the direction of their post on the Ouachita, where
they prepared for a night attack by the invaders. Nolan
passed well to the north of the post, however, pausing only
long enough to write a note to the Fort Ouachita commandant, Vincente Fernández Tejeiro.

> ... I am destined for the Province [of] Texas, and not ex-
> pecting to touch at any of the Posts of your government, I
> have not provided myself with a passport, and, knowing that
> you cannot with propriety permit me to go [through] your
> settlement, I have determined to pass to the North with pro-
> found respect — I have the honor to subscribe myself your
> [obedient] Servant P. Nolan. Thursday Nov. 6, half past 6.

Nolan also sent along a letter to the armed priest who had
accompanied the Spanish troops, ridiculing him for carrying
a weapon.

The Spaniards now commenced a desperate attempt to
outfumble each other in reaching for the weapons with which
to confront the intruder. Tejeiro fired a letter to the commandant of the post at Natchitoches, located farther westward along Nolan's probable route. In it he told of reports
received during the morning of November 6 about an approaching band of armed invaders, of having sent out nineteen mounted militiamen to intercept them, and of their
having come upon Nolan's men "five leagues" from the fort.
The Americans appeared to be so well armed and so resolute,
Tejeiro declared, that his men had not even stopped to speak.
Tejeiro concluded his letter with a promise to assemble more
troops as soon as possible and to lead them himself against
the enemy. He, Tejeiro, would capture that man Nolan —
"tomorrow . . . if I can overtake him." Should he fail in this
endeavor, the Ouachita commandant added as a sort of post-

script, the appropriate officials at Nacogdoches and San Antonio must be notified, so they might take expedient measures to punish Nolan's "audacity."

Tejeiro finished writing his momentous dispatch to Natchitoches about midnight of the same day his undermanned troop had found Nolan. Then the commandant summoned an especially trusted messenger to ride like the night wind, or faster if possible, to Natchitoches, there to give the letter to Commandant Felix Trudeau. With Nolan's formidable army possibly bivouacked somewhere in the dark forest, maybe even on the road between Ouachita and Natchitoches, the messenger's misgivings about departing, even under the night's black mantle, can be imagined; but he started — only to return the next day with his powder flask emptied, carbine smashed, and rations confiscated, and with a tale of encountering ten of Nolan's villains who treated him thus, then compelled him to return to Ouachita. It was a tale later denied by Nolan's men, one of whom speculated that the messenger might have done all this to himself. At the very time of that reported incident, in fact, Nolan kept his men riding all night, to put distance between himself and Tejeiro's fort.

Commandant Tejeiro became so thoroughly alarmed at this juncture that he set out on his own expedition against Nolan, but without success. So, to the original letter that his messenger had striven to carry through the enemy-infested woodlands to Natchitoches, Tejeiro added a note and sent it on to Natchitoches the evening after his man's misfortune: ". . . I believe you have sufficient force to disperse them. If an example is not made, bad consequence must result. I have pursued them the whole day with 50 men but could not overtake them."

At Natchitoches, Commandant Trudeau reacted with similar concern. "I have ordered all the people of the upper districts to assemble and go in search of those Americans," he stated, "until I can gather a sufficient force of militia to overtake them. They have shaped their course above Rocky Creek."

While the Spaniards were showing their consternation, Nolan was enjoying a pleasant trip. Once he had left the vicinity of the Mississippi River and its bordering swampland, the countryside improved in looks and environment, although it was still trackless and uninhabited. Fertile soil nurtured sheltering trees and areas of thick vegetation, which in turn nourished teeming game: bear, panther, and deer. After crossing the Ouachita River Nolan halted his expedition, sent out hunting parties, and with cooked fresh meat renewed their strength and spirits. Then they set out westward again for the Red River, through more "fine country."

Outwardly all seemed serene, but after the brief encounter with Spanish troops some of Nolan's men became apprehensive and began asking questions among themselves. Did their leader really have a passport? If he did, why had the Spanish troops been following them? With the full power of His Catholic Majesty turned loose on them, they mused, three months in this interminable land could prove to be a very long time.

One of the disaffected men, Thomas House, began whispering among the others that Nolan had no passport at all, that they were all in much danger from the Spaniards. Morale sagged noticeably, and Nolan vented his anger on the man who had caused this.

"You are discouraging my party," Nolan warned House. "Be careful not to meddle in this affair, for there is no other law here than blows. If any one flees, Luciano [probably Garcia, a member of the expedition whom Nolan particularly trusted] will catch him, even if he hides in the woods, and will hang him afterwards like a dog."

Another man, Mordecai Richards, asked Nolan frankly about the passport. Nolan spent a great deal of time trying to placate him, Richards claimed later, and promised to appoint him third-in-command of the expedition.

This promotion and the rewards that would ensue were still insufficient persuasion for Richards. Some time later, when most of the men again had been sent into the woods after game, Richards vanished, along with two others. Young Bean thought the three "got lost from our party." Nolan, however, knew better: Richards, a crafty woodsman, would have been among the last in the entire expedition to lose himself in the pine forest through which they had been traveling. A more intelligent guess was that Richards had decided to abandon the risky venture and to flee to the United States, and that he had persuaded the other two men to go with him, even though this meant leaving his own son and his nephew behind in the expedition.

For nearly a week, search parties were sent into the woods to look for the "lost" men; perhaps Nolan thought it wise to mask his suspicion, to avoid suggesting to others by baring his pessimism that it would be wise for them to pull out, too. Then the expedition struck out again for the Red River, and Nolan thereafter kept a careful watch on his men's movements. Furthermore, he began to dole out powder and shot so that the men carried only a few loads at a time, enough for protection and for hunting.

They arrived at the Red River and halted near where

Shreveport stands today, to build a raft. They piled all their goods on the improvised vessel, pushed off, and made for the west bank, swimming their horses. The river crossing carried them still farther into forbidden territory, but Nolan seemed unconcerned, and each man realized by now his own irrevocable commitment to stay. Home was much too distant and the route too obscure to contemplate traveling there alone, or in company with only one or two others.

Four miles beyond the river, Nolan and his men came upon a series of spacious prairies blanketed with buffalo grass, brownish with the coming of winter, and three welcome sights: buffalo, from which they obtained fresh meat; Indians, who were friendly; and domesticated horses, owned by the savages. With the Indians they bartered for new mounts, then rode into the present state of Texas, entering somewhere near where Marshall is today.

Bean wrote:

> In about six days' journey we came to the Trinity river, and, crossing it [perhaps around what is now northern Henderson County] we found the big, open prairies of that country. We passed through the plains till we reached a spring, which we called the *Painted spring*, because a rock at the head of it was painted by the Camanche and Pawnee nations in a peace that was made there . . . In the vast prairie there was no wood, or any other fuel than buffalo-dung, which lay dry in great quantities. But we found that the buffalo had removed, and were getting so scarce that, in three days after passing the spring, we were forced, in order to sustain life, to eat the flesh of wild horses, which we found in great quantities. For about nine days we were compelled to eat horseflesh, when we arrived at a river called the Brasos. Here we found elk and deer plenty, some buffalo, and wild horses by thousands.

The vast Brazos River country where Nolan chose to halt seemed ideal for his purpose: it was remote, comfortably distant from Spanish posts at Nacogdoches and San Antonio, but near Indians Nolan knew as friendly; it afforded timber for cooking and for building, from the stunted oaks, blackjack, pecans, and elms that grew around there, especially in the bottomlands; and with a heavy carpet of grass and numerous streams it attracted the wild horses and other game that Nolan sought.

In January of 1801 Nolan selected for his camp a site on a small tributary of the Brazos. The river, apparently called Blanco in those days, now bears Nolan's name. Between its mouth and a spur of hills Nolan erected a roofless log fort with walls about five feet high, for safeguarding possessions and for protection against possible Indian attacks. Nearby he built other log pens for holding captured horses. The last trace of these crude structures was obliterated long before the first settlers came, and their exact location cannot be positively determined. Probably, however, Nolan's fort was located near the present community of Blum, in Hill County, Texas, some forty miles north of Waco.

The men were weary already from travel, privation, and labor, but their work had only begun: now they must go out after the wild horses.

Exactly how Nolan acquired these animals is not clear. Some, already broken, he probably obtained from Indians in trade. Others he no doubt tamed himself in the Indian manner — after lassoing, choking down, and temporarily hobbling or tying them.

Still other animals Nolan perhaps corralled in a peculiar manner described by J. Frank Dobie in *The Mustangs*: the

animals were walked — not choked — down, to break their
initial resistance.

A group of men, operating in relays, relieved each other in
following a band of horses, at a distance close enough to worry
the animals and to keep them moving on without enjoying
the simple necessities of life: sleep, grass, and water. After
a time the horses became so tired, sore, and sleepy that they
verged on nervous exhaustion. In that state, then, they could
be driven into a corral, fed and watered, broken, and later
driven to market.

Still another method was described by George Wilkins
Kendall in his *Narrative of the Texan Santa Fé Expedition:*

> . . . The white hunters have also a method, which is often
> successful, of taking the wild horses. It is called *creasing,* and
> is done by shooting them with a rifleball upon a particular
> cord or tendon in the neck, immediately under the mane. If
> the ball takes effect precisely in the right spot the animal falls
> benumbed, and without the power to move for several min-
> utes, when he is easily secured. Should it strike too low, the
> horse is still able to run off, but eventually dies.

However it was that Nolan got his horses, he had penned
three hundred of them soon after the completion of his log
stockades. Then he received a friendly visit from two hundred
Comanches, who invited him and his men to partake of Indian hospitality at a location on the "south fork of the Red
River" and to meet their chief there.

The invitation was doubly appreciated. Nolan had brought
provisions for only a three-month journey, and food was becoming scarce. He accepted. Probably he left some men
behind to look after the captured horses, although nothing
was written about this, and it would not have been essential:

the pens probably had been built into the river in such a way
as to allow the animals access to water.

The trip intrigued Peter Ellis Bean. Although he had be-
held many exciting new sights since leaving his home in East
Tennessee, his curiosity had not waned. He observed the
Indians closely, and wrote of the month-long visit:

> . . . A number of [the Comanches] had arrows pointed,
> some with stone, and others with copper. This last they pro-
> cure in its virgin state in some mountains that run from the
> river Missouri across the continent to the gulf of Mexico.
>
> During our stay with this chief, four or five nations that
> were at peace with him came to see us, and we were great
> friends. . . .
>
> These red men have no towns, but roam over these immense
> plains, carrying with them their tents and clothing made of
> buffalo-skins. They raise no corn, but depend alone on the
> chase. Once a year they meet with their head chief on the Salt
> fork of the Colorado river, where he causes all the fire to be
> extinguished, and then makes new fire for the new year; and
> the bands also severally change their hunting-grounds. This
> meeting takes place in the new moon in June. At the place
> where they meet are lakes of salt water, so covered with salt,
> that they can break up any quantity they want.

At the end of a month Nolan brought his men back to their
headquarters near the Brazos. With them traveled a band of
Comanches — part of the group that had entertained them
— who were riding in search of buffalo. At Nolan's fort the
Comanches encamped for a few days, then departed early
one morning. As was typical of Indians, they stole some horses
when they left: to the savages, horse-stealing was more of a
game than a crime, and they could not resist the frequent
opportunities to make off with another man's mount. The

closer they came to getting caught, the greater the honor in
their victory.

On this occasion the Indians stole all eleven of Nolan's
gentle horses, the very ones he used for running mustangs.
Without those animals, he knew, he might not even be able
to return home; certainly the expedition would fail financially.
Nolan and five volunteers — one of whom was Bean — hurried off after the bandits, but with two tremendous handicaps:
they started some distance behind the mischievous Comanches, and they were forced to follow on foot.

For nine days they pursued the culprits. They walked across
vast prairies and forded the streams they encountered, fearing
to halt for long and thus lose their race irrevocably. Finally
they sighted the Indians encamped some distance away on the
bank of a creek. Quietly they approached to within fifty yards
before being noticed. "We went up in a friendly manner,"
Bean said. The savages — four men and several women and
children — stared silently at their approach. The rest of the
men, it developed, were away hunting.

Bean noticed four of the stolen horses grazing nearby. "I
pointed to them," he said, "and told them we had come for
them. . . . An old man said the one who had stolen [the
horses] had taken the others out hunting; . . . and that the
rogue who stole them had but one eye, by which we could
know him when he came. They gave us meat, of which they
had a large quantity drying; and then we were glad to lie down
and rest."

Bean continued:

In the evening, as the old man said, One-Eye came up with
our horses. We took him and tied him, the others saying nothing, and kept him tied till morning. His wife then gave us all

our horses; and we took from the thief all the meat we could conveniently carry. We then told them all that there were but few of us, but we could whip twice their number, and they were of the same opinion. We then returned safely to our camp, and found all in readiness to run horses, and the pen in good repair. But we concluded to let our horses rest a few days.

Judging by their looks, the men themselves needed rest at this time. Many were showing the strain of the preceding hectic months and most had grown beards that were now long and scraggly. They were lank and hungry: Nolan had forbidden the use of ammunition for hunting, apparently keeping it for something more vital than assuaging hunger pangs. By March 17, 1801, they had been subsisting for some time on the flesh of captured mustangs, which were almost as lean as they. In this weakened condition they were to face the greatest trial of their entire expedition.

9. ALARM ALONG THE BORDER

APPREHENSIVE SPANISH OFFICIALS everywhere were expecting
Philip Nolan to appear outside their villages in the faint light
of dawn. They had not received any recent reports about his
whereabouts. Most guessed his strength to be much greater
than it actually was, and they believed his successful disap-
pearance into the middle of their guarded domain could only
herald some well-planned conspiracy, probably involving the
use of Indians, against their established government. None
of them likely would have believed that Nolan's only endeavor to this time had been to round up the horses he had
claimed represented his sole interest in coming to Texas.

Mordecai Richards, who had deserted Nolan along with

the other two men, had contributed to this alarm. After leaving the expedition, the three had fled through the woods to the safety of the Spanish fort at Concordia, across the river from Natchez, where Richards had told the Spaniard Vidal all that he knew, or pretended to know, about Nolan's plans. Later Richards admitted that part of his statement was false, made while under the influence of liquor. Probably he meant to tell the Spaniards what they wanted to hear — or at least something of what they expected to hear — but it alarmed them nevertheless.

Richards claimed Nolan, in trying to quiet his fears about lack of a passport, had said:

> My plan is to follow a Northwestern course, to pass through the territory of the Caddo Indians, and at a convenient place to build a fort for protection against any attacks. Once organized we shall examine the country and look for mines and other valuables which we are sure to find there. We will also go mustang hunting until we are thoroughly acquainted with the country, and obtain the full number of horses we want. Then we shall return to . . . Kentucky, without difficulty, and find friends who are awaiting us. I expect then to receive a commission from the British minister at Philadelphia, under which several of my friends want to go with us to take possession of those lands, or at least to gather their wealth. I am now mustang hunting to procure horses for all of them. Depend upon it; within two years we shall return all safe and rich, since we shall have the support of the British minister, who has already promised it to me indirectly. I am to command the expedition as general, with Mr. Fero as second, and you shall be third in command. . . .

A copy of this "Secret Declaration of Mordecai Richards," dated December 13, 1800, was sent at once to Lieutenant

Músquiz, commandant at Nacogdoches, which Vidal perhaps expected to be the post nearest to Nolan's activity, and probably to other officials. The flurry of correspondence between distant posts became a storm; most of it written that fall and winter, 1800–1801, offered speculation but few facts about Nolan and his intentions. Much of it concerned Nolan's known acquaintances in Nacogdoches and elsewhere: the Leals, Cook, and others. The Spaniards had suddenly lost their *mañana* concept and were busying themselves in tracking down the man they considered the most dangerous individual in their New World.

Military leaves were canceled, militia called to duty. Even the mission life, ordinarily one of surpassing monotony for most people, was changed somewhat. The priest still made his morning round, striding out in the burnished light of a new day to strike the church bell and summon to worship those he himself doubted were the faithful savages, then repeated the function in the jaded red of evening. Between the two tollings he passed out the cheap gifts expected as rewards by his primitive communicants and supervised the planting or the harvesting of crops: corn, beans, tobacco. He continued to make his rounds of the outlying villages to baptize the young and bury the dead in his customary way. Now, however, he listened more earnestly to the chatter of the Indians and noticed who was present, who absent, at gatherings. The noisy clatter of armed horsemen riding along the beaten brown road that passed by the mission disturbed him more frequently, but, fortunately, the riders all proved to be in the service of the King. Almost any instant he expected to see the feared band of Anglo-American outlaws appear over the bald crest of the gentle rise nearby and fall upon him. Under such stress, his intonation of the solemn sentences of mass perhaps communicated more urgency, but he went on calmly with the routine.

Army life was more drastically changed. The military became much more militant in attention to duty. Soldiers of His Catholic Majesty had less leisure now for debauchery, much to the satisfaction of the priests, who were constantly nagging the troops about their low behavior. Time devoted to gambling and drinking fell off drastically. At the same time the Indian women of the neighborhood, whether their status was daughter or wife, relaxed in a somewhat less demanding atmosphere: many of them had lost hours every month — voluntarily or not — entertaining presidio personnel in the time-honored manner.

Now the troops were away much of the time, and when they were riding against an enemy, as currently, they could recoup some of the prestige lost during their disreputable engagements. Although the Spanish trooper had his flaws — he was sometimes a convicted criminal released from prison, frequently irresponsible, often ridden with venereal disease, and virtually always of mere Indian blood, whereas most of his officers were pure Spaniards — he was a hard man to contend with in his rocky, arid, prickly environment. Mere existence demanded that he be a superior fighter and know the intricacies of warfare pertaining to his particular region. Near the presidio he might waste hours in gambling, but away, during a night watch, he never relaxed his vigilance. In placid times he might find nocturnal pleasure and momentary peace with an Indian woman in the woods — or almost anywhere: people knew about those things, after all — but during a march he was careful to avoid an ambush. At home he might drink himself into a blinding fog, but away he had clear eyes or he did not live long.

He could ride all day for many days on rations that would have withered another soldier's stomach. His staples were parched cornmeal, sugar, wheat biscuit, and dried meat, eaten with pepper. Breakfast came early and the evening meal late, but if he grew hungry during the day he stifled his appetite with a piece of biscuit or a drink of water with some cornmeal and sugar mixed into it.

Many of these soldiers in various provinces were joining in the march against Philip Nolan's heretics. In numerous towns the royal army assembled in sun-dappled squares, looked on while robed priests carrying holy water blessed the colors, then rode off. Spiritually, they were as well prepared as they could be; physically, they were obviously imposing: each man had slung a carbine in front of his saddle and sometimes carried heavy horse pistols holstered on each side. Officers bore curved shields, for warding off Indian arrows, with the King's arms colorfully emblazoned on the fighting side.

These horse soldiers thundered out of presidios scattered across what is now the southwestern United States and Mexico: from the west bank of the Mississippi River, along the grassy coastal plains bordering the Gulf of Mexico, and up the sandy Río Grande, all in search of the ubiquitous Nolan and his army that now actually numbered two dozen men. The Spaniards also rode after Nolan's agent John Cook, reported to be fleeing from Nacogdoches to the United States, and they eventually caught him at Rapides. They brought in Antonio and Gertrudis Leal and all other of Nolan's important acquaintances, some of whom were clearly implicated in papers found with Cook.

One such person was Gertrudis, who was questioned at length by the Spaniards and admitted maintaining with Nolan "illicit intercourse as a frail woman." Later Cook and the Leals were to be forcibly removed from the frontier and its opportunities for lawlessness. Cook went to Monclova and the Leals to San Fernando, in Coahuila, where Antonio soon died and Gertrudis used her charms to marry the commandant.

"That man Nolan," however, continued to threaten all of the Spanish domain from some unknown location.

Pedro de Nava's interior provinces headquarters at Chihuahua served as clearing house for the communications traffic. The fact that these messages were long delayed in their horseback transmission across treacherous land and through a devilish climate did not dampen the excitement or ease the alarm. Virtually every day brought a new series of disturbing rumors: two of Nolan's agents and one hundred Choctaws were hurrying westward to reinforce him; the American filibusters might strike at any time — anywhere — by either land or sea; Nolan was bound for the territory west of the Río Grande; the dreaded Comanches, led by "some foreigners," were plotting to attack Laredo; Nolan and two hundred of his American and Caddo accomplices were busy enlisting more Indian allies for a supreme attack on Spanish rule. Considering Nolan's strength and boldness, some Spaniards probably thought it possible he might slash clear through to the City of Mexico.

"Find him!" came the order from above, and it was repeated with increasing volume by every subcommander down the authority chain until, finally, it was boomed into the ear of the underpaid little man who was to be handed the unpleasant task for accomplishment. The big men were thus left free to put their minds into the planning.

"Large columns commanded by officers will not do for reconnoitering the coast and patrolling the country . . ." suggested Governor Elguezábal of the province of Texas, headquartered in the town of San Antonio, to Commanding General Nava. "Small parties in charge of intelligent noncommissioned officers would be more efficient in supplying us with information. The first move slowly, are encumbered with pack animals, are easily observed and avoided; and what is worse, one single reverse, which, if not probable, is not impossible, would cripple our means of action, and perhaps prevent us, in case of emergency, from meeting an enemy of force. On the other hand, small parties, freely overrunning the country, may observe without being perceived, bring prompt intelligence and by resorting to some off-hand stratagems, give time to a large force to act successfully."

The addressee of this ponderous, if valid, observation was, however, commanding general of a rather large territory. The governor considered it wise now to temper his sagacity with some humility. "Should these suggestions fail to meet your approval," he added, his blatancy trailing off, "I request an expression of your views on this important subject, to which I shall be anxious to conform my conduct."

One hundred men under a lieutenant colonel dug themselves in at Camargo, on the Río Grande, to protect northern settlements of Nuevo Santander "from the offensive designs of the Anglo-American Don Philip Nolan." And at Nacogdoches, the troops built a strong stockade around the plaza and mounted artillery pieces there, "capable of making a serious resistance in case of being invaded by any kind of enemies," a description that seemed to admit defeat before the battle was even joined. Patrols rode every day from La Bahía del Espíritu Santo, at the present site of Goliad, Texas, southward across the low plains to the Gulf beach, on the basis of Nolan's early statement that he would follow a southern route. Commanders of militia companies at Refugio, Reynosa, Camargo, Mier, Revilla, and Laredo were ordered to arrest any foreigner who attempted to enter their settlements without a valid passport. Along the Río Grande, continuing patrols were organized that would, hopefully, prevent an intruder from venturing west of that river into the present Mexico. If any of them sighted Nolan, they were to notify each other, unite, and await still other reinforcements. It was a humbling time for the haughty Spaniards.

"The enterprise is certain," the subinspector at San Luís Potosí, Felix Calleja, wrote the Viceroy, "and if the most efficacious steps are not taken, certain will be its success and disastrous will be its consequences. The various Indian tribes with whom Nolan comes in contact will be induced to serve him by the presents he gives them or even without presents by holding out to them the right to pillage. His party, according to reports, consists of fifty armed and resolute men with which number he can easily go through such an open and sparsely settled country without the least danger. . . ."

Weeks passed, and Nolan did not appear on the eastern bank of the Río Grande, or on the coast, or even at Nacogdoches. Maintaining the frontier in such a momentous state of defense had begun to eat inordinately into royal funds, to keep officials away from other duties, and to leave some areas unprotected against other potential enemies. Eventually, most of the militia was excused to go home, but each

man received instructions to keep at his immediate disposal
rations for fifteen days and to be ready to report at any time
for further military duty.

The San Luís Potosí subinspector, Calleja, perhaps a bit
abashed now at the alarm he had imparted to the Viceroy,
speculated in another letter that Nolan's silence could be
attributed to his having heard of the many barricades being
thrown up to stop him. Now, the subinspector suggested,
Nolan was awaiting a more opportune time to strike.

Yet, all the while, Nolan was only adding to his stock of
horses.

The Spaniards sent out agents among the Indians to offer
rewards of up to forty horses for bringing in Nolan or his body
and to spread the information that Nolan was up to no good
— for them or for anyone else. Spanish officials were helped
and perhaps even prodded in this activity by two Nacogdoches traders — and especially by William Barr, who had
felt commercial competition at Nolan's hands some years
earlier and seemed now just as eager as the Spaniards in want-
ing his capture. Barr, who was an Irishman like Nolan, according to a Nacogdoches census, a native of Munster, bachelor, and forty-one, traded extensively with the Indians. He
used this contact to speak to one important chief about Nolan's foul designs.

Characteristically, the Indian carried this gossip directly to
Nolan, who listened with growing anger, then wrote a reply
for the same chief to give to Barr:

> Gentlemen — The Bearer a chief of the Ta-y-as told me
> that you informed him I was a Bad Man, had escaped from
> Prison at St Antonio, that if he saw me he ought not to per-
> mit me to enter his village, — and he has requested this Testi-

mony that he has made the communication to me. — For my part I am at too great a distance to reply to your misrepresentation. — We shall perhaps one Day or other meet & then you will receive the hearty thanks of

NOLAN

Apparently this Indian chief did not inform the Spaniards of Nolan's location. By mid-February 1801, however, firm reports on Nolan's whereabouts finally began coming in from other sources. A letter from Governor Elguezábal to Pedro de Nava provided details.

> San Antonio, March 18, 1801
> Lieutenant Miguel Musquiz, commanding at Nacogdoches, reports that on the 17th ult. [February] the agent of the Tehuacano nation informed him that Nolan was in the vicinity of these Indians' village; and that on the 18th of that month a Caddo Indian told him that he had seen Nolan's trail leading the same direction; and finally that on the 22nd [of February] Paul Bovet Lafitte told him that another Caddo Indian saw three forts built by Nolan above these villages. . . .

Perhaps it struck some high officials as being ironic that of all the Spanish military men on the frontier, Lieutenant Músquiz at Nacogdoches was to draw the lot, one of dubious promise, of going after Nolan, a venture in which, if he were successful, he would win the gratitude of all Spain, including the King himself.

Músquiz was not a perfect commandant, not even a perfect officer. He despised paper work, which was certainly essential to a man's career, and he was otherwise slovenly at times. Governor Elguezábal had spoken castigatingly of him in a letter written December 24, 1800, to Commanding General Pedro de Nava. "That officer [Músquiz] has some of the quali-

fications required for the command entrusted to him," Elguezábal said. "[But] . . . he sends unsatisfactory reports, and
lacks activity in the discharge of his duties. I consider it
necessary to have with him a subaltern officer, able to take
charge of the correspondence, and to advise him."

The first subaltern Elguezábal sent had almost caused two
resignations from the Spanish service — Músquiz' and the
subaltern's. The subordinate's name was José María Moral:
he proved to be infirm — a total cripple, in fact, in Músquiz'
vigorous estimation. ". . . Take him or me away from this
post, or permit me to resign it," Lieutenant Músquiz had
written the governor. At the same time Moral had been engaged in correspondence of his own with the same official,
detailing all the troubles at Nacogdoches, such as the fact that
a soldier named Villafranca was living in open concubinage
with the wife of one Gregorio Mara. "Support me or I resign," Moral pleaded.

The governor had withdrawn Moral — and the soldier
Villafranca, too — and had sent another officer, Joseph María
Guadiana, a surprisingly good bureaucratic choice: Guadiana
was loyal and trustworthy, and was acquainted with the country and its conditions. He was there to handle the correspondence when Músquiz was summoned to eliminate Philip
Nolan.

Judging by the recent performances of Spaniards nearby,
no other officer on the frontier would have even seriously con-
templated this action. He would have preferred, perhaps, to
write thoughtful letters on the subject, or at most to advance
some distance in Nolan's direction and to await reinforcements for a grand assault.

10. THE BATTLE

BEHIND THEM, the eastern sky had turned ruddy in a dawn that flecked the tops of the lofty pine trees with a soft, vaporous light. Westward along a crimson gash that was El Camino Real they clattered: Lieutenant Músquiz and one hundred or more horsemen — sixty-eight were regular troops — riding out of Nacogdoches to track down and exterminate those intruders from the United States. Included among the horsemen was the solemn Nacogdoches trader William Barr, who had volunteered to accompany the expedition as interpreter. Included among the equipment was a fourpounder cannon.

Hundreds of hoofs dug into the damp, red soil, picking up small clods of earth and flinging them some distance backward. The morning quiet had vanished in a din of trampling horses, the leathery screech of saddles in motion, a jangle of cruel spurs, and occasional curses of men who had lost sleep the preceding night to an overdose of poor wine or too much woman.

Lieutenant Músquiz planned to follow this San Antonio road — now Texas State Highway 21 — for a few days, then leave it and strike out across country northwestward, the general direction in which Nolan's stockades had been sighted. He left a diary describing in very brief and dry detail his progress and the events that ensued at the completion of the journey; the book was found more than sixty years later in old Spanish records in the Archives of Mexico by J. A. Quintero, who translated it for publication in the *Texas Almanac* of September 1868. The following information is taken from Quintero's translation.

"March 4th," was his first entry. "Left Nacogdoches early in the morning. Took the road leading to San Antonio, and camped at the Rancho de la Botija."

Músquiz' lack of enthusiasm for writing, one fault of which Governor Elguezábal had complained, became apparent in the diary. Absent was any description of the color or of the excitement or suspense that must have pervaded his expedition; but this can be imagined even a century and a half later. Neither did Músquiz bother to explain a few puzzling details — such as why he needed three days during this urgent period to reach the Angelina River, which lay only some twenty miles distant from Nacogdoches along the road he took. When he arrived at its banks at nine o'clock in the morning of March 7, he found that recent rains had sent the river on a rise, necessitating a further delay: "I ordered some rafts to be made to cross it." By the time that chore had been completed the day was almost gone, so he encamped on the other side. Músquiz seemed to be showing himself as only another procrastinating Spaniard, after all.

At daybreak on the 8th he sent ahead a corporal and six men to repair a wooden bridge on the Neches River, to facilitate the march. He wrote, "Left with the troops at eight o'clock in the morning. At one in the afternoon reached the Neches, and the bridge being repaired, I crossed." This seemed a good partial day's work, but after crossing, Músquiz encamped on the west bank and did not leave the Neches until seven o'clock the next morning: thirty-eight miles in five days.

Perhaps Músquiz should have stayed in Nacogdoches, to attend to the correspondence, and let Subaltern Guadiana lead the men.

Músquiz followed the San Antonio road until about nine o'clock in the morning of March 9, when his location was near what is now the northern tip of Davy Crockett National Forest, in East Texas. From there he took a course "between north and west," and camped for the night on the bank of another stream, which he called San Pedro Creek. Thereafter he traveled just north of due west, and that eventually proved to be a collision course with Nolan.

He was still more than one hundred straight-line miles from the Americans, however, when he reached the densely wooded banks of the Trinity River, probably in what is now lower Anderson County. There, in the morning of the 11th, he discovered that this river, too, was deep and swift-flowing from recent rains, and he ordered a halt while his men built ten rafts. That same evening, when he was well on the other side of the Trinity, six friendly Indians joined him. He recognized them as Tayshas — or Tejas, from whom Texas received its name. The word itself meant "friendly."

Other Indians, however, were less cooperative:

12th At daybreak I sent four volunteers to the settlement of the Tehuacan Indians, on the Brazos river, in order that they might bring with them a captain of the . . . Indians called El Blanco, to show me the spot where Nolan was. The warrior refused to furnish me with the information desired.

For four more days Músquiz led his soldiers somewhat blindly, but correctly, westward. Still he seemed like a lethargic bureaucrat, marching from sunrise until early in the afternoon, when he chose to halt his men and rest. During this time he no doubt rode into the present Freestone County, then cut into Limestone and possibly Navarro counties, on a ranging course. It is certain, by tracking him through his diary, that he went into the present Hill County. "About three o'clock" in the afternoon of March 16 he arrived at the headwaters of the Navasota River, which now lies — and probably even then lay — in southern Hill County, twenty miles or so north of the present city of Waco, Texas.

17th At daybreak I started, course west. About eight A.M. I was informed by the sergeant commanding the vanguard that two persons on horseback had been seen and that they had suddenly hid themselves in the thicket. I sent after them, and they were soon after found and brought before me. They proved to be two Indians. After some questions I asked them, they informed me that there were in that region about twenty-five men, with Nolan; that all of them had long beards; that, if I traveled fast, course west, I would get to the place where they were about sundown. The Indians told me that they would guide me on a route between north and west, so that I could get, without being seen, to the place where Nolan was. They said that the place was between the Monte Grande and the Brazos river. I camped for the night at the Arroyo del Atole.

18th Started at daybreak. . . . Traveled until two o'clock P.M. when I camped close to a spring.

19th Traveled, course north, until about six o'clock P.M. Then I took course west, and stopped on the bank of the Blanco [now Nolan] river. I sent seventeen men with the interpreter, Mr. Barr, to explore the place where Nolan was. They returned before daybreak and informed me that they had found a wooden intrenchment and a pasture-ground, with some horses, on the banks of the Blanco.

At this point Lieutenant Músquiz proved his military mettle. One can visualize other Spanish commanders, especially against the background of recent vacillation, dispatching a swift-riding messenger south to San Antonio, to inform Governor Elguezábal triumphantly that Nolan had been located at last, then to declare that the desperate and dangerous man was said to be well entrenched in a strong fortification which required additional men to overwhelm him. Instead, Músquiz did not even send for instructions. "I immediately started," he wrote in his diary, but he did so warily, as any good commander would.

The next day, at dawn, he encountered two more Indians and from them learned the exact location of Nolan's fort. Músquiz waited until that evening, however, to close the remaining distance. During the night of March 20, he urged his men cautiously forward. Well before sunrise he had his troops in place, divided into three groups, on a hill overlooking the fort. Finally they had the long-sought Americans in their grasp.

•

Inside the fort, Philip Nolan slept, not suspecting the arrival of the Spaniards. He, Ellis Bean, and the four others had returned from the successful trip to retrieve their eleven stolen horses only four days before Músquiz found him.

The others slept, too, with the exception of a few men on watch. Even they were at first unaware of being besieged by an enemy who waited only dawn to scatter destruction.

The spectral approach of Músquiz' troops was first realized by Nolan's captured wild horses, through their remarkable sense of smell. During the night, nickering and snorting and stirring in the nearby horse pens awoke Nolan, and he guessed it meant savages were sneaking up on his horses, to steal them again. He sent a detail to look after the animals. Thereafter he did not hear from his men, but the horses continued to make restless sounds.

In the fort, some men apparently dozed off, but Nolan surely remained awake.

What happened in the next few hours is not really clear. Eliminating obviously self-saving and hero-posing statements from existing accounts, however, these events probably transpired:

In the eerie light of predawn Nolan was able to make out the source of his troubles and their extent. Peering from behind the low log walls of his stockade, he realized that he was being observed from a distance by a large party of mounted men. They were not savages, he knew; many of these men wore sombreros, like that odd lake animal the Indians had once described to him. Now he regretted sending his men outside the stockade to look after the horses: no doubt they had been captured, he reflected — and he was correct. By dawn Músquiz already held five prisoners, leaving Nolan with only nineteen men besides himself to oppose this formidable Spanish force.

Nolan assured himself that all nineteen were awake, armed, and positioned as effectively as possible, and he warned the men to make every shot count: perhaps if they could hold off the Spaniards for a while they might still manage to escape.

"As day broke, without speaking a word, they commenced their fire," Bean wrote years later in his *Memoir*, but his recollection was faulty. Actually, while Nolan strained to see into the dull light of early morning from behind his low-walled refuge, he observed Lieutenant Músquiz' troop advancing on the fort carrying a truce flag, while the remaining Spaniards held their distance. Calling for men to accompany him — probably to make a more impressive appearance — Nolan strode out unarmed from behind his fort and shouted to Músquiz in Spanish: "Come no further, [or] one of us will be killed."

Músquiz halted and summoned his translator, William Barr, the Irish trader. "Noticing that the men who accompanied Nolan were foreigners," Músquiz wrote, "I ordered Mr. . . . Barr . . . to speak to them in English, and to say to them that I had come for the purpose of arresting them . . . that I expected them to surrender in the name of the King."

Barr and Nolan, the two old enemies, then conferred briefly. Nolan told Barr he would not surrender, and perhaps he managed to add an irreverent reflection about Barr's recent note to the Indian chief of the "Ta-y-as" in which he had referred to Nolan as a "Bad Man."

Barr relayed to Músquiz, in Spanish, Nolan's decision to fight, even as Nolan and his companions disappeared behind the wall of their stockade. At that very moment, however,

Nolan discovered he had lost the services of two more men, both Mexicans, who raced from the rear of the fort and eventually scampered across a dim grassy plain to surrender to the Spaniards. One of the deserters had filched Nolan's carbine, no doubt as a potential peace offering, while Nolan had been talking with Músquiz and Barr, and he proudly handed it over to the Spaniards.

Músquiz withdrew his soldiers some distance, behind cover, and the sun rose on a tense scene: Nolan, from inside his fort, urging his men to fight to the death or expect slavery forever after from the Spaniards; the waiting Spanish troops ready to act promptly whenever Músquiz' order came.

"At daybreak, Nolan and his men commenced firing," Músquiz wrote. Whichever side shot first, the battle raged quickly thereafter. Inside the stockade, Nolan rushed recklessly from one position to another, blasting away at the Spaniards with another carbine he had grabbed and shouting to his men, "Make sure of your shots!" From outside the fort musket balls crashed into the logs, but, incredibly, no one was hit. Then, suddenly, Nolan himself pitched and fell lifeless on the trampled earthen floor of the enclosure, shot in the head. The quick Irish blood spread out in a wasted pool.

Bean's *Memoir* described the rest of the fight.

> . . . In a few minutes after [Nolan's death] they began to fire grape-shot at us. . . . We returned their fire until about nine o'clock. We then had two men wounded and one killed [Nolan]. I told my companions we ought to charge on the cannon and take it. Two or three of them agreed to it, but the rest appeared unwilling. I told them it was at most but death; and if we stood still, all would doubtless be killed; . . . we must take the cannon, or retreat. It was agreed that we

should retreat. . . . The powder that we could not put in our horns was given to Caesar to carry, while the rest were to make use of their arms. So we set out through a prairie, and shortly crossed a small creek. While we were defending ourselves, Caesar stopped at the creek and surrendered himself with the ammunition to the enemy. Of the two wounded men, one stopped and gave himself up, the other came on with us. . . . We were so fortunate, that not a man of us got hurt, though the balls played around us like hail.

Fifteen men, including one wounded, were left to fight now, without water, with dwindling ammunition, and with their time decidedly running out. David Fero, the former United States Army officer, had assumed command.

They stumbled into a deep ravine, possibly along the same creek Bean referred to, and huddled there, protected by the steep banks and a nearby grove of hackberry trees. Again the Spaniards closed in, and the Americans fired a deadly volley, forcing the enemy back temporarily. At this juncture, however, the other wounded man crawled out of the shelter and surrendered, pleading for water. Only fourteen men remained, more watchful than ever but with waning hope.

The same man returned to them soon after giving himself up, with a message from Músquiz promising that all Americans who laid down their weapons would be returned to the United States, now that their dangerous leader had been slain. Fero and the thirteen others probably were discussing this development when the trader-interpreter William Barr appeared again under a flag of truce and substantiated the information.

Bean heard his words.

"The commander [Músquiz] wanted us to return to our

own country, and not remain there with the Indians," Bean wrote. "We quickly agreed to go as companions with them." He added that the surviving Americans demanded that their weapons not be taken from them, and he said the Spaniards agreed; but either his memory had failed again or his pride had infringed on honesty. Other accounts, no doubt correct, stated that David Fero clambered out of the ravine first, approached Músquiz, and handed him his knife and pistols. The others followed one by one; later the ten men already held prisoner joined this unhappy group.

Nolan's survivors were led back to the stockade, where the body of their dead leader still lay just as he had fallen in battle that morning. With Músquiz' approval, the two Negro slaves dug a grave nearby. Músquiz, after assuring himself that he had removed all papers from the body, ordered one of his men to cut off Nolan's ears, "in order to send them to the Governor of Texas." When that grisly task had been completed, Músquiz allowed the two Negroes to lower Nolan's body into the primitive resting place — far from Dublin, far from Kentucky, and far from Natchez, where his wife Fanny, with his new-born son, had already come to presume that her husband had deserted her. The Negroes covered the grave, and they left Nolan to lie forever in an alien land.

Now Músquiz acted to send the joyous news of Nolan's riddance to those in higher authority. The trader William Barr volunteered to carry the tidings to Governor Elguezábal at San Antonio, and Músquiz entrusted to him the two ears, all of Nolan's papers, including a diary that has since vanished, and a covering letter.

At San Antonio, the governor read with delight the communication from Músquiz, and no doubt treated the bearer of the message as a hero himself. Immediately, Elguezábal dispatched Nolan's papers and the two ears to Commanding General Pedro de Nava at Chihuahua, along with a covering letter containing a strong recommendation for favor to Barr:

Mr. William Barr, Indian trading agent, has just reached this city, with Lieutenant Músquiz' report, herewith enclosed, of Nolan's death and the capture of his associates, which took place on the 21st [of March].

I forward to you the ears of that American, with all the papers found on his person, which should be examined and translated.

Lieutenant Músquiz' success has been so fortunate, inasmuch as it was accomplished with no loss of lives in his party, that I consider it proper to communicate it to you by express, being convinced that you will be gratified to be apprized of it without delay. I send the same intelligence to the governor of Nuevo Leon, Coahuila and the colony.

When I shall receive Lieutenant Músquiz' circumstantial report, I will forward it to you, and commend to your regard those who have distinguished themselves. [For] the present, I would respectfully recommend to your favor Mr. William Barr, an Irishman by birth, who lives near Nacogdoches. This gentleman, urged by his well-known love [for] the King, volunteered to be the bearer of the welcome tidings.

11. PRISONERS OF THE KING

FOLLOWING THE BATTLE in which Philip Nolan was killed, Lieutenant Músquiz ordered his tired men to make camp near the site of their victory. The sole death resulting from the fighting was, to Músquiz, a most appropriate one. Now, before leaving the vicinity, he gathered the "armament and other properties" belonging to Nolan and his expedition. The list of hardware left behind was not impressive:

    20 Carbines
    2 muskets, one double-barrel and another of
       Spanish arms
    7 pistols
    1 iron shovel

3 English axes
7 iron *Mancas* for horses
1 Mathematics Instrument
3 bullet molds for Carbine and one worm for
  withdrawing wadding from gun

On the morning of March 22, the day after disposing of
Nolan, Músquiz ordered his men to mount, and they began
their return journey to Nacogdoches, with the twenty-four
survivors of Nolan's last expedition — fifteen Anglo-Americans, seven citizens of New Spain, and two Negroes — all of
whom eagerly anticipated an early release to full freedom.

Recent rains had splashed the countryside with varicolored
wildflowers, had brought out the grass in the fertile lowlands
so that it was belly-high to a horse, had left creeks and rivers
brimming. The rains also brought chill temperatures, particularly in the early morning, but spring was definitely in the
air — in fact, had just arrived when Músquiz began his march
back to Nacogdoches — and with the welcome excess of rain-
fall it would be a green one in this often arid region.

On their return trip they traveled east-southeast. They
found the Trinity running deep and out of its banks, and they
were forced to stop on its west side. Concerning this halt
Bean later wrote, fancifully perhaps, "My companions and I,
in a short time, made a small canoe out of dry cottonwood,
which answered very well to carry the soldiers all over. Their
arms and their commander were still on the west [bank]. I
told my companions that we had it in our power to throw all
their guns in the river, take what ammunition we wanted,
and return. Some of them were willing; others said it would
be very wrong now we were to be sent home. . . ."

On April 3 they rode into Nacogdoches — along the same

red-dirt road that led in the opposite direction to San Antonio, under the same pine trees that had caught the first
light of morning as Músquiz' men departed to find Nolan
a month earlier. Into the center of town they rode, and there
the two dozen men of Nolan's last expedition were assigned
"temporary" quarters: "The commandant told us," Bean
said, "he was waiting for orders from Chihuahua to set us at
liberty and send us home." The fifteen Anglo-Americans and
two Negroes were quartered in houses. The seven Spanish
citizens, however, were put in irons and consigned to the
jail, outside of which a sentinel stood continuous watch, because the jail roof was not reinforced and might permit escape.
The King's officers apparently intended to mete out a stern
justice to the Spanish traitors. A guard of twenty men, under
two officers, alternated in watching the other captives, who
soon became anxious about their promised freedom. Only
David Fero, Nolan's second-in-command and a former United
States Army officer, received special treatment: because of his
former status he was considered a prisoner on parole.

For more than a month the men remained in Nacogdoches.
At first they expected daily that release would come; then, as
the time ground on, they began to despair.

Some tried to escape. In the jail, guardsmen discovered
that an iron file had been smuggled into the cell and hidden
there. They retrieved it before the occupants had a chance
to put it to use. Then they found the man responsible for its
introduction and imprisoned him, too, in irons.

On May 18, nearly six weeks after their arrival in Nacogdoches, four prisoners — three Anglo-Americans and a Negro
— had grown desperate enough to attempt an escape, which
they somehow managed to bring off successfully — on foot.

Lieutenant Músquiz dispatched twenty-eight horsemen in three groups to bring them back, but after an eleven-day search no one reported even seeing them. Neither did the Louisiana commandants, who were notified. At Natchitoches, Trudeau said someone reported sighting four men plodding eastward through the woods, but twenty horsemen he sent out failed to locate them.

Encouraged by this success, three more Americans, including David Fero, planned an escape. They solicited outside help and made the mistake of confiding in a local resident who listened to them — then, instead of assisting, reported their scheme to Lieutenant Músquiz, who ordered all three plotters put in irons. As a further safeguard, he shackled most of the rest of the prisoners, too.

The successful escape had marred Músquiz' reputation, however, to a degree sufficient to wipe out most of the credit he had earned for the elimination of Philip Nolan. Earlier Pedro de Nava had remarked, concerning his success, "His merits shall not be overlooked." Now this was all disintegrating.

"I could be no less than astonished at this occurrence," Governor Elguezábal wrote Músquiz angrily. "None of this was necessary." The governor reminded Músquiz of orders he himself had given to insure security of the prisoners and declared that Músquiz could expect to be held accountable for the "serious carelessness."

This warning soon proved accurate. In a letter to Elguezábal, Pedro de Nava grumbled that the escape clearly was due to gross neglect and that it reflected unfavorably on both Músquiz and Guadiana. "Express my displeasure," Nava wrote, "and give positive orders for safekeeping of those still in our hands. I do not share Lieutenant Músquiz' hope of recapture. . . . I have at heart the carelessness of the officers at Nacogdoches."

A month later the lieutenant's difficulties were compounded by a confidential report from Nava to Governor Elguezábal describing how Músquiz and Guadiana lived "in scandalous intercourse, [Músquiz] with the wife of the soldier . . . Juan de la Cruz, and [Guadiana] with the daughter of one Padilla."

With Músquiz' recent brilliance so tarnished, neither Elguezábal nor Nava trusted him any longer with the prisoners, who were ordered transferred to San Antonio. Before leaving Nacogdoches, however, the captives were questioned thoroughly about activities during their time as members of Nolan's expedition. Why had they joined the venture? What was Nolan's actual purpose in coming to Texas? What trading had they done, and with whom? Had anyone — for example, General Wilkinson — supported Nolan's project? Why had the men resisted arrest and fired on the Spanish troops?

On July 20 the prisoners "were seized," as Bean wrote, "and put in irons, and sent off under a strong guard to San Antonio." Although heavily shackled, they were nevertheless escorted by an armed guard of fifty men from the Nacogdoches garrison and fifty others sent out from San Antonio by a distrustful Governor Elguezábal. Even so, David Fero managed to escape at the crossing on the Angelina River, after excusing himself for what he claimed was a call of nature, but he was soon recaptured and returned to his unhappy companions.

At San Antonio the twenty prisoners remained for three months. Then came orders for their removal again, this time to Saltillo, where they were to be met by other troops and taken to the City of Mexico. Heavy rains that sent rivers churning out of their banks delayed their departure, but on November 3 they set out, guarded by fifty men and an officer, through land that, though arid, was blanketed by thick, rough vegetation: small mesquite trees, cactus, and thorny brush and shrubs, which the Spaniards called chaparral. The desolation of this wilderness seemed appropriate to the prisoners' moods: gone were the dreams of a prompt release; the captives were "unfortunate men who [had] put confidence in Spanish promises," as Bean wrote. "These [Spaniards] are a people in whom you should put no trust or confidence whatever."

The Spanish judiciary finally had decided that the survivors of Nolan's expedition were indeed lawbreakers whose immediate purpose had been to rob — horses, certainly, and perhaps other of the King's possessions — and whose secondary objective had been to explore the Spanish domain with the eventual aim of taking some of it for themselves. They were to be considered foreign invaders and not prisoners of war, the ruling declared. This opinion pointed out that most of the prisoners not only had refused to surrender, but had also fired on the royal soldiers and had continued their attack even after Nolan's death. The only question left to answer was where the prisoners should be tried. This was not to be decided for months.

Probably Bean and his comrades were taken from San Antonio southwestward along El Camino Real into what is now Old Mexico. In that country they traveled across more desert, then into the bleak mountains of the interior. Up they climbed, into a cool, dry region, and, eventually, into San

Luis Potosí, more than one mile high. There, on December 4, 1801, they gazed in wonder at imposing buildings, rose-tinted in the waning sun, and at multicolored domes and towers. There, too, they halted, and for months they languished in dark prison cells while the Spaniards continued to debate where to try them.

"By this time we were getting bare of clothes," Bean wrote. "I told [our captors] I was a shoemaker, and would be very thankful if they would permit me, in the daytime, to sit at the door of my prison, and work at my trade."

He continued:

This was granted to me, and also to [one other prisoner]. We made some money; but, in a short time afterward, orders came that we should be sent to Chihuahua. This order was quickly obeyed; and we started on horseback, with heavy irons. Yet it was cheering to think that we were going to change our prisons, hoping that in some change we might be able, some day or other, to escape.

We came to . . . Saltillo, where we were delivered over to another officer, whose duty it was to conduct us to Chihuahua. This man treated us with more humanity than had been shown us before. He took off our irons, and let us ride all the way foot-loose, a distance of four hundred miles. And along the road, and at all the towns, we could look at places, and walk about and see the inhabitants. And we noticed that everywhere they were mixed with Indian, but of a kind and friendly disposition. They were all exceedingly kind to us, presenting us with fruits, clothes, and money; so that, by the time we reached Chihuahua, we began to think we would soon regain our liberty.

Their ride had been a long, hard one — along narrow, winding mountain trails that crossed the Sierra Madre Oriental range; onto the vast Central Plateau of Mexico — an extension of the Great Plains of the United States — which was broken by several mountain systems; then, on March 14, 1803, into Chihuahua, a silver-mining town whose inhabitants ranged from the complacently wealthy to the wretchedly poor. Emphasizing the poverty was a background of elegance: a scattering of richly decorated churches and public buildings, including the royal treasury; fine-dress promenading in the cool, leisurely evenings under trees whose intertwined branches formed a bower above the strollers; fiestas filled with carefree carousing and singing — in Spanish, Italian, French.

Chihuahua was also the headquarters of the commanding general of the interior provinces: Nemesio de Salcedo, who had relieved Pedro de Nava. Salcedo, stern and haughty, ordered the prisoners' declarations taken soon after their arrival. Their statements would then be reviewed by a judge appointed to the case.

At this time, however, the justice process bogged down again. For months Bean and the others waited, painfully, and time again took an interminable turn because of the uncertainty of what lay ahead. Anticipation of early release soured: perhaps, they reflected, the door had been slammed shut, after all.

Except for the anxiety, their captivity was not unpleasant. Within a week after their arrival, they were unshackled, released from prison, and given the freedom of the town during daylight. Their liberty was curtailed only after dark, when they were ordered to report at a designated army barracks for the night.

At this point Bean proved himself an enterprising, ingenious prisoner and a young man possessed of as much charm as his former leader, Nolan, and Nolan's onetime patron, Wilkinson. Through a remarkable bluff Bean was able to set himself up in a profitable business. He told about it in his *Memoir:*

> . . . We received a quarter of a dollar a day for our provisions; but, as for clothing, there was no way provided to get any. Some of my companions got leave of the general to go to other towns to live, but I thought I would find out some way of making something. I gave myself out as a hatter. There was a gentleman who trusted me for whatever was necessary to carry on that business. I employed two Spanish hatters to work with me, for, in fact, I was no hatter at all. In about six months I had so raised my name, that no one would purchase hats except of the American. By this means I got a number of journeymen to work with me. I was clear of debt, and making from fifty to sixty dollars per week.

In these fortunate circumstances one might expect that the poor Tennessee lad who had yearned to see the world would have been happy, especially since he had perhaps found his way into the favors of the town's señoritas. This was not so, at least not now: "It was not possible that I should forget my country, or resign myself to live under a tyranny after having enjoyed the liberty of my native land."

The result of the trial spurred a determination to escape. The judge's decision, announced January 23, 1804, recommended release for all the prisoners. The judgment angered General Salcedo, however, and he immediately overruled it, ordering that the men remain prisoners while the record of their trial was sent to Spain for a ruling by the King himself.

Young Bean began to save his money for a flight to freedom, and he looked around for other prisoners who might be persuaded to risk the attempt with him. By this time fifteen of them had been sent to the presidio of San Carlos, forty miles

distant; the other five, including Bean, remained in Chihuahua. There Bean found a fellow prisoner who indicated a
willingness to gamble with him: Thomas House, who was,
like Bean, a native of Tennessee. Next, Bean obtained permission, under some ruse, to visit San Carlos, with the aim of
secretly enlisting others. He left his shop in charge of a
trusted assistant and departed.

At San Carlos he looked and listened for signs of dissatisfaction, but his observations proved to be disappointing. Most of
the men were "reconciled and happy." Some of them, unaware of Bean's intentions, urged him to join the Catholic
Church, something he would do in time, then to marry into
the good graces of Spain, as they themselves were planning to
do. "They did not expect the general would ever agree to send
us home, as we had come so far into the country," Bean wrote.
"I put them off by promises, but was still making my arrangements to start for the United States."

Unknown to Bean, however, two of the prisoners at San
Carlos — David Fero and a man named Zalmon Cooley,
formerly a United States Army sergeant — had been cor-
responding already with House about an escape, and a few
others were tentatively included. Probably they did not dare
to tell Bean of their plans, because the young Tennesseean
"had gained the good will of all the principal men in [Chihua-
hua], as well as the surrounding villages," as Bean claimed
in his own words. Nor had they told a certain prisoner named
Jonah Waters, whose undisguised fawning in the presence
of his Spanish captors had made them distrustful of him.

A heavy correspondence developed between the two separate sets of plotters in San Carlos and Chihuahua: Bean and
Thomas House, and Fero and Cooley and House. The letters

were carried by messengers whom the prisoners trusted.

From Chihuahua, House wrote Fero that his guns were in good trim and that he had laid up a variety of supplies, including fish hooks, lines, pinole, and water bags for the trip. "All keep a parte," he urged them, "for feir of suspicion." He enclosed a leaf from Philip Nolan's journal, which had somehow found its way to the middle of a dusty Chihuahua street, where an Indian had found it and turned it over to one of the Americans.

Later House wrote again. "Sum say our papers is gon to Spain But I Donte Beleave it the Ginral may have sente his opinion with the judgmint But I think the Jinral will Desid on it him self Simon [McKoy, one of the prisoners] says he sees a grate Bundel of papers on his table which makes me Beleave he is at work on them."

House requested Fero and Cooley to let Bean in on their plans. "I am not a fraid of him informing on me," House wrote, then added in another letter, "He is industros and will be of sarvas to us."

The date originally set for their escape, March 22, was postponed, apparently to await a ruling from Salcedo on their latest move to obtain freedom: a petition requesting their early release from captivity. The correspondence continued, however, and in one letter House wrote, "This comes By the Hand of a friend . . . Give him a little Brandy and he will fech any Rightings Safe you give him And he has a handsome wife and hir I shall [have] Before he Returns She is a Kind pretty Creature. . . ."

Within a week House fell ill, possibly from a malady passed on to him during his impropriety, and again the plans for escape went awry. House pleaded with his companions to wait

for him. "Don't leave me for love of humanity . . . ," he wrote
Fero, "[for] if you [leave] me I shall think you ungratful and
I shall be lost a mung the Bruts."

Then a letter Bean sent to House resulted in the final destruction of all their plans. Bean had located two Spanish
soldiers willing to desert — a common military offense in New
Spain — and to join the Americans in their venture. Jubi-
lantly, he wrote House a letter specifying a meeting place and
a time for the start — on a specified day "at an old church"
— and the letter fell into the hands of Spanish authorities,
delivered to them by the treacherous Jonah Waters, who
somehow intercepted the letter, read it, and gave it over, all
in a further attempt to ingratiate himself with his captors.
Without warning or explanation Bean was arrested, confined
in a dungeon in stocks, then, on the following day, was shackled
"with two pairs of strong irons" and left in a drab, lonely cell
to reflect on his predicament.

Routine search also uncovered House's incriminating letters, which were destined to be preserved even to this day in
archives, and other correspondence showing that Fero had
been communicating with a resident of faraway Nacogdoches
about his plans for escape. Furthermore, questioning of other
prisoners provided some damaging testimony, especially from
Waters and the sole remaining Negro. After that, House,
Fero, and Cooley were imprisoned, too.

The strength of the evidence against House and Fero left
them no maneuvering room; both admitted they had planned
to escape. Bean and Cooley, however, denied planning this.
They claimed they had only told House they would accompany
him; actually, both men declared, they had no intention of
doing so.

Salcedo remained skeptical of all four men. He ordered them kept in prison. There they waited in despair while more months crept by.

During the ordeal Bean observed someone in even greater distress than he: his friend and fellow captive Joel Pearce, a young North Carolinian. Bean related the experience in his *Memoir*:

> . . . They brought into my prison one of my companions, who was at the point of death. . . . He was taken sick at a place some distance off, and requested that he might see me before he died. As the catholic religion obliges them to comply in such cases, he was brought to me. But my poor, unfortunate countryman did not expect to find me ironed and in close confinement. When the prison-door was opened, he saw me, came in and sat down, and said to me: "I never thought to see you in this place; but, though it is a prison, I shall not leave you until I die, which I expect will be in a few days. . . . I shall die in the company of a countryman."
>
> . . . He continued with me for five or six days . . . daily growing weaker. During this time, I forgot my prison, and thought only of my sick friend. By this time he was able to converse with me but little. . . . [Then] he died, and was carried away to be buried. . . . I was more distressed in mind than ever, thinking it would soon be my time to suffer the same fate.

Instead, however, Bean one day found himself freed from his chains and his gloomy prison cell, and once again allowed the freedom of San Carlos during daylight hours. Now, however, he wanted to return to Chihuahua: he had learned that the illness of his friend Thomas House had become progressively worse, and he wanted to visit the ailing man. His travel request was approved.

In Chihuahua Bean visited with House, who advised making

the escape without him, "as it was impossible that he should ever go." In the same town Bean looked up Jonah Waters, the man who had been responsible for his recent confinement. "I had it in my power to have taken his life," Bean wrote, "and in a manner that would not be discovered; but, though he was a man of such meanness, I thought it not right to take his life without giving him a chance. I challenged him to fight with equal arms, but he refused, and would not see me."

Bean was not a man to be put off this way. He found a sturdy stick and searched for Waters until he found him. "I told him I must have some satisfaction. He began to beg off, but I gave him no time to excuse himself. I fell on him with my stick, and beat him severely, and left him with two women. . . ."

Bean heard nothing from the Spaniards about his breach of the peace, for a reason that was later suggested by the American soldier-explorer Zebulon Pike. In 1807 Pike, who happened to be another protégé of General James Wilkinson, was also captured by the Spaniards during an expedition and taken to Santa Fé and Chihuahua. Later, however, he was released, after having had an opportunity to talk with some of Nolan's men. Upon his return to the United States he wrote an account describing the conditions of the prisoners, and of Bean's enemy he said:

> [Jonah] Waters, of Winchester, Virginia, a hatter . . . carries on his business at Chihuahua, has embraced the Roman Catholic faith, after betraying a well concerted plan of his companions to escape, . . . in which it is supposed they would have succeeded; his treachery caused them a close confinement in irons, and in a loathsome prison for three months — he is hated and despised, not only by his own countrymen but by every honest Spaniard in the place.

Because of their betrayal by Waters, the four frustrated prisoners — Bean, Fero, Cooley, and House — were still in Chihuahua when the Spaniards brought Pike there, and they heard of the explorer's own misfortune and the background of it. General Wilkinson had sent him on two probing expeditions into newly acquired lands after the Louisiana Purchase, in 1803, had added an expansive territory to the United States: 885,000 square miles extending from the Mississippi River to the Rocky Mountains, from the Gulf of Mexico to Canada. The area had been purchased from France, after Spain had receded it — including, of course, New Orleans — in 1800, in a secretly signed Treaty of San Ildefonso, another of the frequent intrigues between those two countries. Spain had given the territory back, for certain considerations, on the condition that France would not sell it to any nation but Spain. France immediately ignored this part of the treaty and sold the vast area to the United States for about fifteen million dollars.

Following Pike's return from his first expedition into the West, Wilkinson had commissioned him to lead an exploring party through the center of the Louisiana Purchase. So, in 1806, he had discovered the celestial Rocky Mountain peak that bears his name today, then later had encamped on what he said he thought was the Red River.

The river was, instead, the Río Grande, in the territory of the highly suspicious Spaniards, who were still alarmed by frequent rumors of other expeditions like Nolan's: first, one supposedly led by a man described as Nolan's brother, then, another said to be commanded by one of the four men who had escaped Lieutenant Músquiz at Nacogdoches. Now these rumors gave way to the unmistakable presence of a group commanded by an officer of the United States Army! Immediately, the Spaniards arrested Pike and his men, but they masked their feelings behind the usual polite exterior, treated their latest captives with much consideration, and prepared to send them on their way to the United States. Nevertheless, when they welcomed Pike into their homes and public buildings, they hid their maps from his view.

At Santa Fé the governor interviewed Pike in the spring of 1807, and Zalmon Cooley served as translator. Later, at Chihuahua, Pike talked with David Fero, who risked Spanish displeasure by slipping away from San Carlos for an unauthorized visit. The explorer recalled that both Cooley and Fero — former members of the United States Army — pleaded with him to campaign for their release. Pike, himself the son of an army officer, was especially moved by Fero's appeal. "This man," he wrote in his journal, "had formerly been my father's ensign."

Pike addressed a request to General Salcedo urging the release of the prisoners; in it he emphasized that all of the captives had presumed that Nolan entered Spanish territory with a passport. Salcedo replied that the records had been sent to the King for action, and he must await the decision.

At Chihuahua, Pike's hosts showed him a carbine they said was Philip Nolan's — the same weapon, possibly, that had been filched by the two deserters shortly before the battle commenced. Before leaving, Pike also heard something about the activities of Peter Ellis Bean, and he wrote a description, brief but sufficient, after he had returned to the United States in July 1807.

Ellis Bean, of [Grainger] County, state of Tennessee, a hatter, formerly carried on his business in the city of Chihuahua, but being detected in an intrigue with the daughter of an offi-

cer, and refusing to marry her, was in close confinement at
[San Jerónimo], a few leagues distant, in good health.

Bean did not mention the affair in his *Memoir*. He wrote,
instead, of his despondency at this time. "We had passed five
years, in all, in Mexico," he said. "Our cases in this time had
gone to Spain; and had also been sent to the United States,
and laid before Mr. Jefferson, at that time president — who
said he knew nothing of us, and that we should be tried according to the Spanish laws. This showed little humanity or
feeling, thus to give up to a nation more barbarous to her
prisoners than the Algerines. But what can a poor prisoner
expect, when the leading men of his country fail to see justice
done him? . . . As Mr. Jefferson did not know us, and had no
expectation of being benefited by us, it was less trouble to say,
Hang them!" Bean commented that hanging — "a momentary pain" — would have been preferable to remaining in
prison, but that the Spaniards had no feeling for their acute
distress.

Then, suddenly, it appeared he might be given fulfillment
of his wish for an early end to the misery. Early in November
1807 — six months after Pike's departure — Bean and eight
other prisoners were rounded up and crowded together in a
Chihuahua barracks room. There they were held without
explanation for days. Every waking hour was filled with speculation until one day two priests visited them and offered to
hear their confessions. The portent seemed unmistakable,
but they were not ready for such finality. Instead, they asked
the priests to return the following day.

"All our conversation that night," Bean wrote, "was about
our being put to death."

In his *Memoir* Bean wrote further of the anxiety of this time and, incidentally, indicated the extent to which he had fallen in Spanish esteem — no doubt as a result of the romantic "intrigue" Pike had reported:

> Soon the next morning the priests returned, and David Fero asked them if we were to be put to death. They said they did not know — perhaps some might be. I then began to conclude it would be me, and all my companions thought the same thing. . . .
>
> All that day [after confessions] the talk among us was . . . who it would be. I told them . . . that if the thing went according to justice, and they hung the worst man, it must be [Jonah Waters], for he was, without doubt, the greatest villain, and ought to have been dead some years ago. Waters sighed, but said nothing.

The priests' visit and the anguished speculation that followed had in fact resulted from recent receipt of the King's decree, dated in Spain, February 23, 1807, regarding the fate of the prisoners — and of their lenient judge, whom the King commanded to be removed from the bench, but who had died — no doubt fortunately — since ordering the prisoners released. The captives remained unaware of this edict, however, until the day following the priests' second visit, when, on November 9, a representative of General Salcedo read the fateful document to them. Accompanying the Spaniard on his visit to the cell were the defense counsel and the prosecutor.

No detailed account of the event exists, but the drama of the moment can be easily imagined: the bewilderment and anxiety of the nine men as their door was flung open and the uniformed Spanish officers appeared, the rising apprehension felt by the prisoners as they were instructed to kneel for the reading of the decree, their awe as the dreaded words hit them. One of every five men, to be determined by chance, was to be executed. The rest of the captives were to be punished with hard labor for a period of ten years. Only the surviving prisoners who had fired on the King's troops from inside Nolan's fort were to participate in the fateful lottery. The others, captured before the fight began, were to be excused from this agonizing part of the sentence.

The nine men to whom the decree was read qualified for inclusion in the lottery. No others survived: deaths and escapes had reduced the number to this. Since the total fell short of ten, local Spanish authority, in a surprisingly generous decision, ordered that only one man must die. The method of selecting the individual who would forfeit his life was left to the prisoners themselves to determine.

They decided on dice, to be thrown according to their ages: the oldest man would throw first, the youngest last. The prisoner who threw lowest would be the loser.

Aptly complementing these macabre arrangements was the grim equipment for playing the game. The captors brought into the room a drum, a blindfold, a crystal tumbler, and two dice. Then they blindfolded the oldest man, Ephraim Blackburn, who was about forty, and led him to the drum. They told him to kneel beside it, to take the crystal cup in his hands, and to shake the dice free so that they would roll across the face of the drum. When he completed this maneuver, the awed onlookers saw the dice thump to a stop at three and one, making four. Then Blackburn learned, to his dismay, what a low number he had thrown.

The next man threw three and four: seven; the next, six and

five, eleven. David Fero threw five and three: eight; Zalmon
Cooley, six and five: eleven. The much despised Jonah
Waters rolled six and one: a very lucky seven.

Three men were left. "And so we went up, one by one, to
cast the awful throw of life or death," Bean wrote. He would
be next to last to throw.

The man before him threw four and three: seven.

"I took the glass in my hand," Bean said, "and gained the
prize of life, for I threw five." The dice showed four and one;
he had barely escaped execution.

The last man threw five and two: seven.

"My poor companion, who threw four, was led away from
us, surrounded by the clergy, to be executed the next day."
Actually the date was November 11, 1807 — two days later —
when Ephraim Blackburn was hanged, in the Plaza de los
Urangos, in Chihuahua. He had wandered far from his
Quaker faith, and shortly before giving up his life to the
King of Spain he allowed the priests to baptize him into the
Catholic Church.

The surviving members of Nolan's last expedition were
assembled in the plaza before a gallows and forced to watch
their companion's death. The trap dropped from beneath
Blackburn and his body fell to a jerking, final halt "in the
presence of many sorrowful hearts that beheld it."

More than six and one-half years had passed since Blackburn and his comrades had fought the Spanish troops. Perhaps some of the others now reflected on Nolan's last instructions that day: "Fight to the death! The Spaniards will make
slaves of us all for life."

"The rest of us were returned . . . to prison," Bean wrote,
"without any other notice; and we so remained three or four

days, when orders came that some of us were to be sent away, and I was one of them. The next day the governor came and told us that I and four of my companions were to be sent to the South sea, to a place called Acapulco, and that we had first to go to [the City of] Mexico." Actually, three others would make the trip with Bean; more perhaps followed later.

Most of the other prisoners were to vanish forever behind the prison walls. Eventually Bean was to be able to call himself the last surviving member of Philip Nolan's last expedition, and he would be the only one of these prisoners to return to the United States. By that time, however, fate would have made him a man without a country in every respect.

12. A "DOUBLE TRAITOR"?

DURING THE YEARS when Peter Ellis Bean was being held in various Spanish prisons, General James Wilkinson, in the United States, was having his own troubles — in courts of justice.

Two months before Ephraim Blackburn was hanged in Chihuahua, Wilkinson's onetime friend Aaron Burr had been tried in Richmond, Virginia, on a charge of treason. Although Burr had been acquitted of allegations that he had conspired to break up the United States for the establishment of his own empire in the West, and of plotting to engage his country in a war with Spain for personal gain in Mexico, the trial resulted in his final fall from public favor. This meant, for him, the bottom of a decline that had been accelerated several years earlier, during his last year as Vice President, after his slaying of Alexander Hamilton in a duel that had grown out of Hamilton's public criticism of Burr.

Wilkinson had not been on trial in Richmond with Burr — in fact, he was the chief witness for the prosecution — but the proceedings proved to be perhaps more damning to him than to the accused, because of certain incriminations that were publicized as a result of the trial. For understanding the details some background is required.

Wilkinson had known Burr for years. Both the careers and the personalities of the two men showed certain parallels. Both had enlisted during the Revolution and had been commissioned in reward for outstanding service. Both reached lieutenant colonelcy about the same time.

Both men also complained of slow promotions, became dissatisfied easily, and frequently ranted against superiors. The Conway Cabal, aimed at the replacement of General Washington, attracted both: Wilkinson became involved in it, of course, as had been shown by his loose talk at Stirling's dinner in Reading, Pennsylvania, and Burr was almost persuaded to participate actively in the same plot, because of his dislike of, and lack of respect for, Washington. Both told their listeners whatever they thought those people wanted to hear — especially when it would further ambition — without regard for honesty. Both possessed talent and capability, but dreamed selfishly of schemes and promotions that not only proved to be impossible of fulfillment, but that finally caught them in their own webs.

Their strongest affinity, however, became noticeable in the years immediately following 1800, when Burr showed evidence of looking to the West for his fortune, as Wilkinson already had done.

Burr, after killing Hamilton, needed a new direction. He became an outcast among Americans — to whom Hamilton became a martyr — although he was at that very time serving out the last part of his term as Vice President. One of his bitterest enemies during this unhappy period happened to be the President, Thomas Jefferson, whose hostility had been aroused in the preceding election, when Burr practiced what Jefferson thought was an attempted swindle to take the Presidency, after Burr had campaigned for the office of Vice President. With the election over, Burr used a peculiarity of the ballot to contend that his supporters had voted for him as President, not as Vice President. The Electoral College gave Jefferson and Burr seventy-three votes each, passing the decision to the House of Representatives, which eventually chose Jefferson.

After the fatal duel with Hamilton, and after Burr's sagging political and personal reputation had collapsed, he evinced his great interest in the West. What his ultimate intentions were, however, never became firmly known.

One fact was obvious: his relationship with James Wilkinson became close, although Wilkinson tried to hide this association to avoid alienating his powerful supporter and Burr's enemy, President Jefferson. Wilkinson and Burr visited one another occasionally, and these meetings logically led to rumors that the two were plotting some sort of conquest in the West — something many men dreamed of in those days. In Washington the French minister, whose duty it was to observe and to report on such activity, said that Wilkinson was "devoted" to Burr.

Many other sensational stories spread as to Burr's actual intentions, and some of them mentioned his planning to seek help from Great Britain, which was, as usual, interested in any scheme that would weaken the United States. Corroborating the rumors about Burr to some extent were the various exploring parties dispatched by Wilkinson, after he had become military commander of the northern section of the Louisiana Territory, to probe into the newly acquired possessions beyond the Mississippi River — notably the two commanded by Zebulon Pike and another by Wilkinson's son James. These expeditions all seemed to have been the General's idea, but they also attracted the interest of President Jefferson.

Activities of the late Philip Nolan also had provided corroboration. Wilkinson, it seemed, had taken more than a patron's interest in Nolan's journeys through Spanish lands. Although the General himself had not ventured into this hazardous region, he knew it well through the descriptions given by Nolan and others. Speculation had it that he was passing on all this information to Burr, perhaps for a price.

After 1805 Wilkinson had been in an even better position to gather data. That year he received an appointment as governor of the Louisiana Territory. The new office, combined with his military command, gave him broad authority in the West and enabled him to work more effectively and in greater secrecy with Burr. A few people even were to claim that Wilkinson was the instigator of the western plot, but this was all unsubstantiated talk. In fact, nobody could offer any concrete proof that either man was actually engaged in conspiratorial scheming of any sort. Only Burr and Wilkinson knew what was passing between them.

As it developed, Burr definitely was plotting something for

his own gain in the West, and he began raising money for recruiting and equipping an army. He visited Spanish and British ministers in Washington to solicit help, some said, from either of those nations. He planned a visit to the Mississippi Valley and New Orleans, from where he could have a closer view of the situation and where he might enlist further support. In 1805 he commenced a journey down the Ohio from Pittsburgh, where he was supposed to have met Wilkinson before his departure. The General's arrival was delayed, however, and Burr went on: he would meet Wilkinson later, at the General's headquarters in St. Louis.

Wilkinson overtook his friend near Fort Massac, however, and there the two conferred off and on for four days — about what, no one really knew, of course, except the two men themselves. An officer attached to the fort later noted in his diary that Wilkinson and Burr devoted some time to walking by the river, engaged in "animated" conversation, but the officer was unable to hear their words.

After four days Burr continued down the river to New Orleans. Prior to his departure Wilkinson wrote him a cordial introduction as "a great and honorable man" to Daniel Clark, Jr., one of the most important citizens of New Orleans, and provided Burr with comfortable quarters on an army boat bound downstream.

The General soon had reason to regret his generosity. After Burr's arrival in New Orleans, Clark reported to Wilkinson that the city was abuzz with rumors of Burr's intention — to carve his own empire out of the western United States — and that Wilkinson was said to be supporting him solidly.

Wilkinson had underestimated the public's capacity for deducing what was going on, as he frequently did. He was dismayed to hear his name openly linked with such a plan, and in the future he became more discreet. Nevertheless, Wilkinson received another visit from Burr when the former Vice President, returning home up the Mississippi Valley from New Orleans, stopped in at the General's St. Louis headquarters.

Within a year Wilkinson lost his post as governor of the Louisiana Territory — and his valued window on the West — by antagonizing the citizens of St. Louis through certain arbitrary measures that forced President Jefferson to replace him. He retained his military command, however, and actually gave up little of his importance in a developing border situation: war with Spain once again threatened on the southwestern frontier, and Wilkinson was ordered to that area. He had established his headquarters at Camp Claiborne by October 9, 1806, when a messenger arrived from Burr with a coded letter for the General. It was dated the preceding July 29, and it was in reply to a letter Wilkinson had written earlier requesting additional information about his plans. In his answer Burr presented in detail the progress he had made, including plans for British ships and perhaps even United States Navy vessels to appear at the mouth of the Mississippi River in support of western conquest.

As Wilkinson decoded the letter, however, he must have realized Burr could not possibly succeed in his scheme for empire, however it was meant to be set up. So, despite a promise contained in the letter — "Wilkinson shall be second to Burr only: Wilkinson shall dictate the rank and promotion of his officers" — the General seems to have felt that the best course for his own preservation lay in exposing the whole plot. Furthermore, his standing with the administration had been slipping, and it appeared he might even be on the verge of replacement. He determined, then, to notify President Jefferson of what Burr was planning, but he spent nearly two weeks getting a letter off to Washington about it. He also sent Jefferson a copy of the decoded letter, implying, of course, that he had done nothing whatever to encourage Burr to promise to make him second-in-command of the enterprise.

Then Wilkinson raised a one-man bellow along the Mississippi Valley: Burr was coming, he announced, bound downriver for New Orleans, which he intended to capture as part of his western plot. President Jefferson ordered the alerting of forts along the Ohio and Mississippi rivers to the menace, and instructed them to intercept Burr if they saw him. Wilkinson went to New Orleans, where he began preparing for an attack and ordered martial law for the city — because, he said, Burr had many sympathizers there — and quickly antagonized the inhabitants with his extralegal measures.

Wilkinson's frenzied warnings were of course ridiculous; they were a screen to cover his true role. Burr and a few companions were indeed bound downriver for New Orleans, but the former Vice President intended his trip only as a visit similar to the earlier one — for planning and for enlisting the support of influential persons. His greatest infraction was to throw out hints regarding his plans to people along the way. When he learned of Wilkinson's preparations against his arrival, however, he left the river and tried to flee eastward. Authorities apprehended him in Alabama in February 1807.

The news of Burr's arrest reached Wilkinson about the same time the General's wife, Ann, died of tuberculosis, and Wilkinson was unable to exult over it. With Ann's death he lost his staunchest admirer and the one person on whom he perpetually leaned for support, and to whom he was always faithful. For all his promiscuous dealings, his fidelity to his wife was strong and — despite a few rumors to the contrary — no doubt constant. Still, even in his sorrow the nation must be considered, and Wilkinson stiffened to devote himself to the Burr problem.

By betraying Burr, some people were to speculate later, Wilkinson probably believed he could profit in several ways. He could win favor from Jefferson, who of course detested Burr. He could display his staunch patriotism for all doubters to see. He could even help his old friends from commercial days — the Spaniards — who might have lost a slice of territory had Burr been successful in the West. Finally, he could wiggle out of a now-unwanted involvement in a plan whose certain failure would result in his own downfall — and of course in Burr's. By sacrificing Burr, then, Wilkinson could not only save himself but perpetuate his good name.

Wilkinson's strategy thus resulted in Burr's arrest and trial on a major charge of treason, by allegedly plotting to split up the Union in making himself king or emperor of a domain in the West. The General, who was the prosecution's chief witness, arrived at the trial site, Richmond, Virginia, a month late, and in the meantime nothing could be accomplished in his absence: without his testimony little proof, or none at all, was available. His only major item of evidence, in fact, was the coded letter. The General finally arrived on June 13, 1807 — a day when Richmond was broiling in a humid temperature of nearly one hundred degrees. Despite the heat, he was full-uniformed — in a cut that was, as usual, of his own design.

In court Wilkinson's eyes met those of Burr for the first

time since he and Burr had discussed their plans. "I saluted the bench," Wilkinson wrote President Jefferson later, "and in spite of myself my eyes darted a flash of indignation at the little traitor . . . the lion-hearted, eagle-eyed Hero, jerking under the weight of conscious guilt, with haggard eyes in an effort to meet the salutation of outraged honor. . . . He averted his face, grew pale, and affected passion to conceal his perterbation."

Some other accounts of the meeting differed. They described Burr's eyes as being the ones that flashed indignation; but Wilkinson's story was the one that Jefferson read. The General followed this up with vituperative testimony against Burr. Later, in his *Memoirs*, he was to record some of his comments.

. . . Whether the design was to sever the union, or invade Mexico, a war with the Spaniards on the Sabine [which Burr hoped for and which Wilkinson could have created had he chosen to do so], would have removed the army out of the way, and given a full scope to the conspirators. If Colonel Burr's design was to sever the union, Spain, at war with us, would gladly have aided him; — if to invade Mexico, the war would have furnished a most desirable pretext, and thousands would have crowded to his standard.

. . . I could hardly believe, that the man whom I had so long loved as my friend, and whom I had so long admired as a soldier, a statesman, and a patriot, could bring himself to engage in so criminal and detestable an enterprise . . . — an enterprise, in which the plunder of our own citizens, at New Orleans, was to prepare the means for the plunder of the Mexicans; and the invading and conquering [of] Mexico, was an operation of such magnitude, that I doubted whether funds

could be provided to meet the expense; or whether the conspiracy could be matured and ready to burst, without the
countenance or connivance of my own government. . . .

. . . My friendship with Colonel Burr, was formed, while he
was a gallant faithful soldier of the revolution; when his heart
was warm, and his hand was ready in the cause of his country;
— and when he was associated with the most pure and gallant
spirits, in the noblest and best of causes.

To witness the showdown between Wilkinson and Burr,
hundreds of visitors jammed Richmond, and most of them
expected — hoped in fact — to see Burr hanged. The end of
the long trial brought for Burr a verdict of not guilty, however,
and for prosecution witness Wilkinson a figurative guilty verdict, by clearly exposing his prior relationship with the defen-
dant. Andrew Jackson labeled Wilkinson "a double traitor, a
man who betrayed his country and perjured himself about it
afterward."

Wilkinson's friend Thomas Jefferson — to whom the General once referred, in one of his frequent piques, as "our fool"
— was as disappointed with the verdict as Wilkinson. During
the trial, when much abuse had been heaped on the General,
Jefferson had written Wilkinson, "Your enemies have filled
the public ear with slanders, and your mind with trouble . . .
The establishment of their guilt, will let the world see what
they ought to think of their clamours . . . No one is more
sensible than myself, of the injustice which has been aimed
at you. Accept, I pray you, my salutations and assurances of
respect and esteem."

Despite the failure to establish Burr's guilt, the trial in-
stigated by Wilkinson completed the man's ruin. The former
Vice President, that "gallant faithful soldier" of Wilkinson's

former acquaintance, lived a life thereafter painful in its length — nearly three decades more. No doubt he had planned to invade Mexico — others too, of course, had talked about doing so — but many people also had become convinced of his designs on the Western Country of the United States.

For several years Burr exiled himself to Europe, where he continued to try to attract the support of foreign powers for his western plan. Then he returned to the United States, but not to happiness. A favorite grandson died, then a beloved daughter, then Burr himself — on the same day his second wife divorced him.

Despite Burr's acquittal, Wilkinson proclaimed that his action against the man had saved the Union, by exposing the conspiracy. He also claimed to have saved Mexico for Spain, and he was careful to let the Spaniards know of this valor even before the trial. To the viceroy in Mexico City, Don José Iturrigaray, Wilkinson dispatched a military aide with a letter describing the plot he had just shattered. Then, before the officer's departure, the General also instructed him to look over the country closely while en route, for the preparation of a map.

In his letter Wilkinson warned Iturrigaray of a continuing threat to Veracruz and Mexico City, and, incidentally, included a statement of costs he said he had incurred in trapping Burr. A reimbursement of $112,000, he claimed, would cover his expenses. He concluded with an observation that he was putting his reputation on a block by his letter to a foreign power — obviously with the hope that his daring would hasten payment.

Unlike the Spaniards of Wilkinson's commercial acquaintance, however, Iturrigaray was not impressed. He answered Wilkinson's letter with polite thanks for the "righteous intentions" and sent the General's emissary back with empty pockets. From the United States government, however, Wilkinson recovered eleven thousand dollars to cover his "expenses" during suppression of the conspiracy — a figure that, incidentally, allowed $1750 for the cost of preparing a topographical map of the route to Mexico City, based on his aide's trip.

Coincidentally, this was during the period when another of Wilkinson's men — Lieutenant Zebulon Pike — was being held in Mexico after having been arrested by the Spaniards on the banks of the Río Grande. Some time after the return of the emissary, Pike heard of his visit, without knowing that the man represented his own superior and patron, Wilkinson.

"We this day learned that an American officer had gone on to the city of Mexico," Pike wrote in his journal April 20, 1807. "This was an enigma to us inexplicable, as we conceived that the jealousy of the Spanish government would have prevented any foreign officer from penetrating the country; and what the United States could send an authorized agent to the vice royalty [for] when the Spanish government had at the seat of our government a charge d'affaires, served but to darken the conjectures."

Pike, an officer of vast integrity, probably did not have a sufficiently suspicious turn of mind to guess correctly: that both he and the "American army officer" he heard about were indirectly involved in activities that would later be regarded as shadowy, when some historians would suggest that Pike's expeditions into the West had been dispatched by Wilkinson preparatory to putting Burr's plot into operation. Pike later denied, no doubt honestly, that the General had even hinted of this purpose to him, but Wilkinson would have kept such an intention to himself.

The Burr trial opened the door to further questioning of Wilkinson's character, ability, and discretion. The following years saw a series of courts called to investigate his conduct: a court of inquiry and two courts-martial before his military career had ended. In all of them Wilkinson was a lion, loud and quick in attacking those who sullied his honor, following the advice his father had given him years earlier. Wilkinson always asserted that he welcomed the investigations, and he expressed eagerness to volunteer all the evidence in his possession.

The clamor for an investigation of Wilkinson came first from the jury foreman of the Burr trial, Congressman John Randolph of Virginia, who despised the General personally and the military generally. Randolph, a sarcastic, eccentric man who could be inconsistent in his beliefs, nevertheless was firm in his hatred of fraud, corruption, and pretense. This was a characteristic that perhaps explained his affection for the simplicity of children, and no doubt explained why some of his colleagues in the House of Representatives hated him. Randolph was convinced not only that Wilkinson was the epitome of cheap fraud but also that the rumors of his being in the pay of Spain were true: thus he was a traitor as well. As proof he displayed some correspondence between Wilkinson and the man now known to be a Spanish agent, Thomas Power, that indicated the probability of Wilkinson's having received Spanish money. In December of 1807 Randolph asked the House to look into the General's activities.

Wilkinson reacted typically to this needling: he called for a court of inquiry himself, and Jefferson, whose administration was being embarrassed by these frequent attacks on its military favorite, complied with his request.

The court convened in January of 1808. Wilkinson defended himself with his usual bombast.

Much of Wilkinson's present difficulty had evolved from his unfortunate habit of alienating friends. This time it was Daniel Clark, Jr., the New Orleans businessman, who had turned on him because Wilkinson had undercut him in some loose after-dinner conversation by declaring that Clark's wealth was not what reputation had made it out to be. Wilkinson's remarks were relayed eventually to Clark, who determined to have revenge.

Still, Clark did not consider himself safely equipped to engage in a campaign of diatribe against anyone, and especially not against a mudslinger like Wilkinson. Some aspects of Clark's private life, particularly his excessive weakness for beautiful women, left him open to attacks on his own character; so he worked through John Randolph, supplying Randolph with evidence that pointed to Wilkinson's guilt.

In retaliation, the General heaped his abuse on both men, after he had determined that Clark, too, was involved. In his *Memoirs* he wrote, "I can distinctly trace the source of my persecutions . . . to the celebrated John Randolph of Roanoke, who is entitled to all the credit, to be derived from the cunning, zeal, perseverance, and perfidy, displayed in his complotting against the character of a man [Wilkinson], whom he feared and hated." Of Randolph's informer he said, "In Mr. Daniel Clark, of New Orleans, [Randolph] found a congenial spirit, every way qualified for his purpose . . . This gentleman who had always been my professional friend and obsequious servant, as his correspondence will testify, was suddenly converted into a remorseless enemy, and the world remains to be informed, of the causes of this sudden revolution in the conduct of Mr. Clark."

In the court of inquiry Wilkinson admitted receiving Spanish money, but said it was all in payment for tobacco shipments made years earlier, while he had been engaged in his commercial venture. He presented as evidence a statement from those years, in Philip Nolan's handwriting, accounting in detail for money received. Despite the incriminating letters Randolph had waved around Washington, the military court accepted Wilkinson's testimony, largely, it seemed, because of army camaraderie.

In an opinion rendered in July 1808, the court declared itself satisfied that Wilkinson "had been engaged in a tobacco trade, with Governor Miró . . . before he entered the American army, in 1791; that he received large sums of money, for tobacco, delivered in New Orleans, in the year 1789; and that a large quantity of tobacco was condemned, belonging to him, and stored in New Orleans, in that year; but it has not been proved, and after the fullest investigation, and comparison of testimony in the possession of the court, it does not appear, that he has received any money from the Spanish government, or any of its officers, since the year 1791, or that he has ever received money from the government, or its officers, for any other purpose, but in payment of tobacco and other produce, sold and delivered, by him or his agents."

In its opinion the court also remarked that the correctness of Philip Nolan's statement of account was "highly probable," but that it did not really matter: "if [General Wilkinson] did receive the money, as stated, the transaction was fully justifiable, and if he did not receive it, there is no proof of his having received it at all." The court found no evidence of Wilkinson's having received a Spanish pension — and said, in fact, that the General seemed to have served his country with integrity.

Congressman Randolph attacked the purpose and the partiality of the court and refused to appear there as a witness against Wilkinson. He asked, instead, that Jefferson provide the House of Representatives with War Department files on the General for an investigation of its own. Jefferson countered that most of the papers had been burned in an 1800 fire, a statement that was true. Jefferson was, however, otherwise evasive, and Randolph fumed.

Wilkinson exulted: his honor had been vindicated — a decision of which he had never really been in doubt — and his antagonists had been subdued again.

"Having passed the ordeal . . . and repelled the calumnies of Mr. Randolph and his confederate, Mr. Clark," he boasted, "I flattered myself, the vengeance of my enemies had been exhausted and that my persecutions had terminated."

This proved to be largely true, but for only a few years.

13. DISMAL EXISTENCE

In Mexico, the vengeance taken by Peter Ellis Bean's enemies continued without interruption. When Bean's companion Ephraim Blackburn was executed by order of the King, seven years and two weeks had passed since Bean left his relatives in Natchez without explanation or goodbye, six and a half years since he had received Lieutenant Músquiz' pledge of release to return home.

For a while after his capture the future had held some promise: hope fed his spirit. Each day had sapped a fraction of his optimism, however, until he had long ago sunk to an emotional low point. Then his inherent resilience had come to his aid. Bean's spirit was too strong to permit him to grovel for long in black despair. This was evident in his *Memoir*, even considering that it was written years later and that it contained some clear exaggeration as to his finer qualities. His hardihood was even more obvious, however, in his survival of a long life of captivity: he was a self-sustaining man, and he had a remarkable talent for adjusting.

All his strength was to be required for a new ordeal. He and the other survivors among the group for whom Blackburn had died now found themselves sentenced to "hard labor." To serve out the penalty Bean and three other prisoners were transferred to the "place called Acapulco," on the "South sea," there to be imprisoned in the gloom of the Castillo San Diego, which was even then more than a century old.

Their trip to confinement would be arduous, with virtually no hope for escape. From Chihuahua they were to travel southeastward to Mexico City, more than eight hundred miles away. From there they would proceed two hundred more miles, in a direction south-southwest, to Acapulco, the oldest port on the North American Pacific coast. Into Acapulco came vessels carrying Oriental silks and spices from the Philippines for transshipment, overland by way of Mexico City and Veracruz, to Spain; but the excitement of observing this strange new place would not be Bean's to enjoy.

He and the other three prisoners were escorted out of Chihuahua in mid-November 1807, heavily shackled and accompanied by twenty-five horsemen. The only real comfort allowed them for the trip were "easy-going" horses that the guard commander had provided. They retraced some of the route they had followed on the trip northward from San Luis Potosí: down the Central Plateau, through yucca- and cactus-covered desert country to an area that gradually grew greener with every slow mile, then back into the mountains. At every village through which they passed, curious inhabitants gathered around them and stared; most of the people had never before seen an Anglo-American.

Despite their ignorance the natives displayed a strange amiability. "Of those that came to see us," Bean said, "some gave us money, and others sent us provisions. They were all mixed with Indian, and showed us real friendship, and seemed to have humanity in their hearts. The Spaniards were hardhearted and barbarous, and seemed to have no other feeling than to make us as miserable as possible."

At Salamanca, about two hundred miles from Mexico City, they rode upon a high, fertile plain and into a village dominated as usual by the church domes. There they were deposited in a high-walled plaza and left largely to themselves, since they were still safely shackled. Once more a curious, friendly crowd gathered to stare and to talk.

The visit again proved Bean's masculine charm, which had already been demonstrated at least once — or perhaps it was his ability as a storyteller that showed itself. In his *Memoir* he related an intriguing occurrence of his Salamanca visit.

From out of the crowd, he said, appeared a woman who asked him, in a low voice, if he desired to escape. Bean, perhaps suspicious, replied that it was impossible, that he had resigned himself to fate. The woman whispered a promise to free him from his irons, then she vanished.

Surprised and curious, Bean asked a man nearby if he knew the woman with whom he had been talking. From this stranger Bean learned that the woman's name was Maria Baldonada and that she was the recent bride of a very rich, very old man. "This brought me to study," he said, "what she meant by telling me that she would free me."

Night came, and he retired to previously assigned quarters,

which opened on the plaza. There he had been furnished a thin mat and a blanket. He stretched out on the mat, but he could not sleep; people continued to mill about outside, and he observed them idly through the open door.

Suddenly he noticed the woman named Maria walk to the part of the plaza where she had spoken to him earlier. Accompanying her, Bean noticed, was a man wearing a long cloak.

Bean called to her in Spanish, a language he spoke fluently by this time, and she walked over to where he lay, gracefully seated herself on the mat beside him, and in the familiar low voice informed Bean that the man with her had brought files for cutting off his irons. He should walk slowly and inconspicuously into the square, she said, and stroll to a certain horse stable, one that she designated. There, out of sight of the crowd, the man would file off the shackles. Another man, waiting outside the plaza, would toss a rope over the wall for Bean to climb, and the same man then would lead him to her residence, where he would be safe thereafter.

Bean answered that his absence, when it became apparent, would no doubt result in even greater suffering for his three companions, and that it would not get him what he really wanted: escape from the country. He was much too far from home, he knew, to be able to make his way back.

The woman urged him to reconsider. "I have horses and money," she said, "and you can have anything without exposing yourself to be retaken. I have several haciendas, in any of which you can stay without its being known."

While they talked time ran out. Bean was summoned to dinner by his guards. Before he left, however, the woman whispered to him that he should think further about the proposal she offered. On the following morning he must visit her, she insisted, and she quickly gave him directions for finding her.

After that Bean could think of little other than what Maria had said to him. "During all that night my mind was so much occupied with what I would have done had I been by myself, that I could not sleep. . . . I . . . reflected that the lady was married; and if her husband should find out that she was the means of getting me away, it might . . . be the cause of my being retaken."

Morning came, and with it new determination: Bean asked for and received permission from his captors to visit a store, in the company of a soldier, to make a small purchase.

He bypassed the store, however, and with the slow-thinking soldier still accompanying him, he hurried to Maria's residence, where he found her waiting at an open window. There he gave his official escort money to buy a drink somewhere nearby — a bribe that almost invariably worked with these troops — and promised to wait for the man's return.

When the soldier had left, Bean heard Maria Baldonada say in her persuasive manner, "Now is the time for your freedom. . . . I have a safe place to hide you, and you will give the soldier money to make him desert . . . you must know that I can do it, for they all love money, and have none." Then she became even more enticing: "You need not think, because I am married, I am bound. . . . About a year [ago], I was married to a man fifty-five years old, in order not to displease my father and mother. He is a man of great property; but I can venture to tell you I do not love him." She spoke of how their own lives could be different, if he accepted her offer.

This prospect surely was appealing to Bean, but he continued to reflect on the suffering he might thus cause his companions — or so he wrote in his *Memoir*. He also mentioned a flicker of hope still stirring within him for release from captivity. Possibly his greatest consideration, however, was what might happen if he were caught. He had survived an earlier ordeal brought on by his affection for the comely, dark-eyed women of this country, as Lieutenant Pike had reported, and this time any punishment likely would be much worse.

Bean mused over the eventualities, and when the soldier returned he "[bade] adieu to the lovely Maria Baldonada" and returned to his companions. Soon afterward they saddled their horses and left Salamanca, but Bean immediately regretted not risking the chance to escape, utilizing the beautiful rescuer. "I was unhappy," he wrote of the hours following his departure, "and could not pass off the time as usual." His regret was to be even more pronounced the next three years, during days that proved to be as dismal as they were long.

Within a week after leaving Salamanca they looked down upon the fabled Valley of Mexico, from the height of their mountain road. In the center of the valley sprawled the City of Mexico, its streets laid out like a gridiron, populated by one hundred thousand people. Here was the capital of the wealthiest province in New Spain, and its appearance, even from a distance, was one of ostentation: mansions, churches, and public buildings were clustered around the center of the city, and their colorful domes glittered in the deepening yellow sunshine of late autumn.

Once they had descended from the mountains, however, all the allure disappeared. Bean and his three companions were placed for safekeeping in a compound already jammed with three hundred other prisoners. Fortunately, they were held there only a week; then they began the last part of their journey, southward across more mountains to Acapulco. There they again had their first view of the city from heights overlooking it, but this scene was much different from that of the Valley of Mexico. Beyond the horizon stretched the blue Pacific Ocean, as calm as its name implied, at least for the moment; below, along a lush strip of land separating the curving shoreline from the encircling mountains, lay the town. They saw an almost landlocked harbor and, on a hill near its entrance, the grim Castillo San Diego, protected by a hundred guns and thick stone walls. The fort had been built in the seventeenth century as a defense against pirates, but Bean was to remember it for the rest of his life as a supremely somber prison.

They rode down a narrow mountain path, through the town, and up the hill to the fort. There they clattered over a bridge that crossed a moat and, once inside, they dismounted. Their "voyage" from Natchez, from the Nolan River, from Nacogdoches, San Antonio, San Luis Potosí, and Chihuahua, had finally ended, and they were still shackled.

An officer called out each man's name. When Bean answered to his, he was ordered to step forward, still in his irons, and to follow another officer, who conducted him to his cell: a dark room, three feet wide and seven feet long, whose stone walls reflected a dim finger of light that poked in feebly from the far end of the room through a small, barred opening built into the thick wall of the castle. The door swung shut behind him, and Bean surveyed his plight. Probably at this moment he again regretted losing the chance to go with Maria Baldonada at Salamanca.

Looking around, he saw one other opening in his cell: a door window, perhaps three square inches in area, also grated. He peered through that, and observed that a soldier had been stationed just outside. From the man Bean learned that his three companions had been imprisoned together, in a larger cell.

Hours passed tediously; the light from the small outside opening grew even fainter. That evening an officer unlocked the cell door and brought in some of Bean's possessions, along with a mat for a bed, and food: beef, bread, and a pot of water. Bean asked why he had been separated from his companions, and the officer replied that this was done on orders from Chihuahua: Bean was considered a dangerous man, and he must be guarded with care. Then the door slammed shut again, and Bean was left alone in the blackness of a particularly dismal night.

At nine o'clock the next morning he heard the door open once more and saw the same officer enter, this time to examine his irons. Bean now requested that he be allowed to join his three companions, but the officer refused: he spoke again of the orders to keep Bean isolated. "I tried to content myself as well as I could," Bean wrote, "though there was but little happiness to be found here."

Still, he shook off abjection and thought over the possibilities of escape. "But seeing the strength of the walls, and having nothing to work with, I concluded it was impossible . . . and [even] should I succeed, I would have to travel three thousand miles through their country to get to the nearest part of the United States. As for the distance, I cared nothing about it, if I could only break through those walls."

So he continued to hope, and one day he took advantage

of a friendly, talkative guard to buy a small knife. With this tool he began to chip away at the monstrous wall. Any activity, no matter how futile, seemed better to him than none at all, and perhaps it helped him maintain his balance. His digging was unsuccessful, of course, but his spirits held up, and he continued to hope.

Three months passed for him this way. Mostly they went by in total silence, with the only variation in the wearing monotony being the arrival of beef, bread, and a pot of water, and the inspection of irons. Eventually, however, he did find a companion, which he wrote about with dramatic simplicity:

This place lies in sixteen degrees of north latitude, and is very warm. There is here a lizard — which the Spaniards call *quija* — which is about nine or ten inches long and about three inches thick. It is as white as snow, and, if you hold it between you and the light, you may see the bones in its limbs and body. One day, as I was lying on my mat, I saw one of them, for the first time, on the wall. Watching him, I saw that he was trying to catch the flies that had come into the prison when the door was opened, to get out of the sun. I did not know whether he was poisonous or not, but I determined to feed him. So I caught some flies, and put them on the end of a straw I had pulled out of my mat; these I slipped up the wall to him, and found he would take them off the straw. This was my amusement for some days, when he became so gentle, that he would take flies off my hand. Every morning, as he came down the wall, he would sing like a frog, by which means I had notice that he was coming. In about a week he was so gentle, that he did not leave me at night, but stayed with me all the time. Every day, when they would open the door to come and examine my irons, he would get frightened, and hide himself under my blanket. When the door was again shut, he would come out and stay with me. I found that he was sincerely my friend: in fact, he was my only companion and amusement.

Bean had suffered through almost a year of this agony when he learned that one or two of his companions had been sent to the hospital for treatment.

This gave him an idea. Casually he questioned his guards about the location of the hospital and learned that it was half a mile distant — in town, as he had hoped, and not in the fort. Again he began to contemplate an escape. All his plans started from the hospital.

One day, when the guard officer was making his rounds, Bean lay back on his mat and complained of feeling unwell. The officer promised to send a doctor, then left. When Bean heard the door swinging open again he quickly struck both elbows against stones in the floor, increasing his pulse rate to a point so high that the doctor, upon examination, ordered him sent to the hospital. This eventually gave him another chance to escape.

In his *Memoir* he wrote a dramatic, though artless and perhaps in places exaggerated, account of it.

They sent an Indian, who carried me . . . on his back. When I got [to the hospital], although I had two pairs of irons on me, they put my legs in the stocks. They consisted of two large, hard logs, having each two half-circular holes . . . so that the top one shut down on the other. I found that, with the irons and stocks, there was no chance of extricating myself. In addition to this, there were ten thousand *chinces* biting me day and night. So I resolved the next day to say that I was well, and return to my castle. But, in the evening, I was taken with a violent fever. I suppose it was caused by my removal from a place where there was no air, to one where there was too much.

It was about twenty days before I began to recover. In this time it had become very sickly in the town; and the hospital was so crowded, that my room was filled. There was a man laid on each side of me. One of them died . . . about three hours after he came, and the other that night. The next morning two more died close by me. I began to think that, in a few more days, it would be my time, but I still improved.

In all the time I had been in the hospital, my allowance was two ounces of bread in the morning, with some gruel; and the head of a fowl and some soup for dinner. As I began to recover, I had a great appetite, but my allowance was not increased. I had money, but was not allowed to purchase. One day a [priest] brought me a hen's head, as usual. As I was almost starved, I was in a very ill humor, and would have destroyed myself, but for the reflection that I should let Him take my life who give it to me. I took the plate as he gave it to me, and asked him why it was that my share of meat every day was the head and neck. He answered me, in a very short manner, that I must eat that, or go to hell for more! I flew into such a passion, that I rose and threw my plate at him, and hit him on the head, and, as the priests in that country have their heads shaven, hurt him very much; and as I happened to be out of my stocks at that time, I sprang to my water-pot and threw that at him also, but unfortunately missed him. Being very weak, the effort to throw the pot . . . caused me to fall on my back; but I got up again as well as I could, and got back to the plank where I lay. . . . I had scarcely sat down, when the sergeant of the guard came in, and put my head in the stocks . . . where I was kept for fifteen days. My only regret was, that I did not kill him; as they would then have taken my life, and put an end to my sufferings.

While my head was in the stocks, the *chinces* ate all the skin off my neck, for I could not help myself. When my head was taken out . . . I told them I was well, and they might send me to the castle. The doctor had my irons taken off . . . , and in their place a chain of about fifteen pounds' weight was fastened to each leg. By wrapping [these chains] around my waist, I could walk very well, though I was weak.

I thought I would try to escape on the road to the castle, for there were but two soldiers guarding me, and they were armed only with sabres. I started off with them, and had got about three hundred yards from the hospital, when we came by a house on the outside of the town, having a large garden. In this house the woman sold a kind of small-beer. As I had money with me, I asked the soldiers if they would drink some. They quickly agreed to it. We went into the house, and called for some. She brought it out, and we drank it, and called for some more. I asked [a soldier] to go with me into the garden, which he did. I walked with him . . . and found a large bunch of pinks, which grow in that country as large as roses. I asked him to come and see those fine [flowers]. He came, and, in handing him one, . . . I caught him by the neck, presenting my knife-blade, . . . and told him if he did not give up his sword, I would kill him. He quickly obeyed. . . . I told him I was going off, and, if he would go with me, there would be no danger of being retaken. He said he must do so, or he would be put in prison in my place. I saw, however, that he was unwilling. I then gave him a dollar, and started, telling him to go and buy the worth of it in bread for the journey, as we had no provisions; and that I would wait for him at the burying-ground outside of the town. So I left him, and went out at the back of the garden, and, before he could let the officer of the fort know it, I was safe in the woods.

By means of a steel I had to strike fire, I cut off my irons, and ascended the side of a mountain, so that I could see all the town and castle. I sat down in a shady grove, where the singing of birds and the thought of being at liberty so charmed me, that I was as happy as any monarch. The sweet-smelling blossoms, interwoven with the shade, formed for me a palace; and, though I had been starved in the hospital, I did not feel hungry, nor was I weak. I felt strong and happy, and sat in that pleasant shade till night.

I then made my way into the town, and went to a shop, where I supplied myself with bread, bacon, cheese, and a large gourd of brandy. As I was passing near the door of another shop, I heard two men speaking English. . . . As they came out, I spoke to them, and found that they were Irishmen [from] a privateer, which had that day come into port from the city of Lima. I asked them what sort of a man their captain was, and if they thought I could talk to him. They said they would conduct me to the house [where he was staying], and ask him if he would be kind enough to have some conversation with me. They did so. He sent me word to come to his room; and when I went in, he asked me of what country I was. I told him I was an American. He could hardly believe me, as I spoke Spanish as well as he could. I told him I wanted to go in the brig with him, and that I had been a prisoner such a [long] time. He said he would clear me from that place, but . . . I must go away and take care of myself till the next night, and then go on board the brig and hide myself well: he would then sail, and I would be safe.

I went to the woods that night, and spent all the next day in listening to the songsters of the forest, being greatly pleased. When night came, I went where the sailors were to meet me, and found them waiting. . . . They gave me sailors' clothes, and I went on board like a jolly tar, thinking I was safe. That night we broke the head out of a water-pipe, and at daybreak I took up my abode in it. There were about three hundred such pipes on board.

About ten o'clock next day a guard came and searched the vessel, and, as I was not to be found on board, they returned to the shore. The vessel was to sail in about two hours. There was on board an old Portuguese cook, who knew I was concealed, though he did not know where. The old wretch fell out with some of the Irish sailors, and went ashore, and told the governor I was hid on board the vessel; that he saw me, and heard them knocking on the hoops of a barrel. The poor Irishman was arrested, and told that I was a king's prisoner, and, if he did not show where I was, they would send him to prison. They frightened the poor coward so, that he told them I was on board, and he would tell where I was. They came with him on board, and he showed them the water-cask in which I was concealed. It was rolled out, and I was well tied, so that I could not move. I was then thrown from the vessel down into the boat, which bruised me badly, though no bones were broken. I was . . . landed and carried to the castle again, where my two pairs of irons were put on me, and I was placed again in my little cell. I consoled myself with the thought that I had enjoyed a few hours of liberty, and had heard the birds sing, and perhaps might hear them again.

After some reflections upon my hard fortune, my mind became easy and I thought of my poor companion the lizard. As I had just come out of the light, it was so dark I could not see anything. The next day my lizard came down the wall, and, as soon as I saw him, I reached out my hand for him . . . but he was afraid. . . . I gave him some boiled beef, and he ate it; but when I wanted to take him, he ran up the wall. It was four or five days before I could get him to know me; then he was as friendly as ever, and was the only companion I had.

Again, however, Bean proved to be incapable of resigning himself to abject inactivity, even in the stark gloom of his surroundings. He conceived a plan to provide release at least temporarily from his stifling environment; he would buy liquor and drink himself into a stupor.

From his mat he procured strips of palmetto and began weaving them together. Within four or five days he had fashioned a cord perhaps ten yards long — of sufficient length to reach the grasp of a pedestrian walking past his small cell window that opened through the outside wall of the castle. Then he posted himself at the window straining to peer outside it, and waited. Soon he saw a woman approaching, and he called to her. She stopped and asked, "Where are you?"

"You can't see me," Bean replied. "I am a prisoner, and I wanted you to do me a favor." He told her he wanted "some spirits."

The woman paused, then agreed to try to help him. Bean tossed a few coins out the opening, instructed the woman to tie the purchase onto a cord he would have strung out waiting for her return, and watched, hopefully, as she walked on.

Then he got his palmetto line, tied a chunk of mortar to one end of it, and threw it out the window. The other end of the line he tied to his arm; and he sat on the floor, with much anticipation, "like a fisherman waiting for a bite." With him was his lizard, which he had named "Bill."

After a time he felt a tug on the line and heard a woman's voice say, "Pull. I am going." Bean stood and carefully inched his prize upward. When it came into view he saw that it was a cow's bladder, filled with liquid. Slowly he worked it through the bars of the window, then eagerly took a drink. He had stretched himself out on his mat with Bill, feeling warm and relaxed for a change, when he heard a noise outside his cell door. Quickly he hid the bladder, and saw an old priest enter.

The man had heard stories about Bean's pet lizard and had come, out of curiosity, to see him.

"I took [the lizard] in my hand and played with him," Bean said. "The old [priest] observed that it was in the power of man to do anything, if he would but turn his attention to it. He then gave me some money, and left. . . ."

Alone again, with only the speechless lizard for company, Bean took another swallow from the cow's bladder and lay down: indeed man did have power, and ingenuity. Soon Bean was past the pain of his dismal existence.

"I can truly say that, during the year and five months I stayed in this cell the last time," he wrote later, "the hour I was drunk, and unconscious of everything, was the only happy time I saw."

14. FREEDOM AT LAST

PETER ELLIS BEAN'S remarkable confidence afforded him, in time, still another opportunity to escape.

One day when the guard officer was visiting his cell during a routine examination Bean listened in on a discussion between the officer and a sergeant. The talk concerned work to be done: the officer spoke of some rock-blasting required, and the sergeant replied that none of his men knew how to set a charge.

Bean volunteered for the job. He had learned about powder and guns from his kin in Tennessee. "I told them, quickly, that was nothing — that I could do it to great perfection." Several days passed and Bean presumed that his offer had been ignored. He had, in fact, forgotten about it, when the same sergeant suddenly entered his cell one day to say he had been given approval to use Bean for the work.

"You see," said the sergeant, ". . . I have befriended you; and if you act well, perhaps you may gain more privileges. But I am sure you won't try to get away, as I have done this to get you out."

Bean voiced his concurrence, but secretly he thrilled at this new chance to flee the deadening stone walls of his prison. "I was constantly thinking of the chance I had lost at Salamanca . . ." he said. "As soon as the sergeant told me this, I was sure I would escape, or be shot." To finance his effort he still had about one hundred fifty dollars, brought from Chihuahua, which the Spaniards had allowed him to keep.

His irons came off, to allow him to work, but in their absence long chains were secured to each of his feet. To walk he was forced to wrap the chains around his waist. Then, escorted by two soldiers, he proceeded to the work site, where he observed — with growing hope — forty or so other prisoners guarded by only half as many soldiers.

Bean was allowed access to the "gallery" of a nearby residence for preparing his explosives, and he promptly used the opportunity to charm a woman who lived there. Secretly he gave her money to buy him twelve knives, and through another sympathetic soul he arranged for the purchase of two pistols. To this arsenal he somehow added twenty-nine cartridges. He asked his accomplices to keep these weapons until he found a chance to use them.

Bean wrote another dramatic, though crude, account of what transpired:

That night I began to talk to some of the prisoners, and told

them it was in our power to escape; and, if they said the word, it
should be done. I was to wait till the next day for the answer of
the chief one among the prisoners. The next morning, as we were
going out, he came to me, and said some of them would go if I
would give them notice. I told him that afternoon was the time;
. . . I was determined to make a start, and if any one wanted to
go, when they saw me take a basket of stones on my shoulder to
[the place] where the prisoners were [shoveling] dirt, they must
be ready; that I would give them twelve knives to distribute among
them; that I should try to take a gun from a soldier, and all must
do the same, and not to run until we had the soldiers [fleeing],
which would be in less than ten minutes after we began. The
pistols I was to get were to come at that time, as the man who was
to bring them was to give them to me on the way.

So we got to the place. I went to the house, where I got my
cartridges and the knives. The latter I gave to the man who was
to give them to the prisoners. He put them in his basket; and,
after a short time, he gave me the sign that he had distributed
them. I arose and asked the corporal if I might carry some baskets
of dirt, to exercise myself. He granted [my request]. I started and
filled my basket with broken stone, and went to a soldier. All the
prisoners were waiting for me to begin. I asked the soldier to
strike me some fire. As he was doing it, I took a stone out of my
basket and struck him on the temple. He fell; I took his gun,
dropped my basket of stones; some were running. The soldiers all
fled — there was not one that stood.

. . . Seeing a reinforcement coming from the castle, and all the
prisoners gone, except a few cowards that were afraid to [escape],
I started off with an old Spaniard, who had come with us from
Natchez. I saw that he ran very slow, and halted and fired, telling
him to go on. He ran about fifty yards, and came back with his
hat full of stones, to help me fight. The other prisoners were gone,
but the Spaniard and I made [the soldiers] retreat. I then told him
he must go, that I could escape; but if I left him behind, he would
be taken. He . . . [ran], and I thought he was gone; . . . but in fifty
yards more I met him. . . . "Where are you going?" [I asked]. . . .
"I have come to help my old friend," [he replied], "and have

brought more stones." I told him there were too many soldiers, and we must go. By this time they fired at us. I exchanged shots with them, and the old Spaniard threw stones. The next fire, a shot [hit him]. . . . He . . . said: ". . . make your escape; but, before you go, shoot me, for I would rather be shot than taken." But, as I could not do this, I started, with the bullets singing around me, and finally escaped from them with my chains on.

After I ascended a mountain, I sat down, greatly fatigued with the race and battle. I felt so much distress for the loss of my old friend the Spaniard, that I forgot I had my chains to remove. . . .

After sitting awhile, I began to think of my chains. I had a razor and my old knife-blade: these I struck together and made saws, with which I [finally] removed my chains. . . . After this was done, I walked along the mountain, to listen if I could hear any of the prisoners taking off their irons; but I could hear nothing. I then sat down on a rock, regretting the [certain] death of my old friend. And, [while] I was thinking what I should do, and which way I should go . . . I saw a soldier coming up the mountain. I caught up my gun, and started to charge on him. . . . When he saw me, he said: "You must not shoot me, my friend. My name is Corral . . . and, as I saw you had made your escape, I came in search of you to go with you." . . . We then sat down on a rock, to consider what was best, and what course we should take. It was impossible to travel through the woods, [because of] the thorns and vines. . . . By this time, night was coming on; and we went down the mountain, where I got water, for I had nearly given out for want of it. We then took a road for a small village called Cojucan, to the west of Acapulco. We travelled that night till my feet blistered, and the skin came off . . . for, until that night, I had not travelled any for two years. We stopped just at daybreak, in a thick wood, close by a cattle-ranche; and soon . . . saw a man coming through the woods, with a large gourd on his back. I called him, and . . . asked him how far it was to Cojucan. He said it was nine miles. Thinking it best to make some arrangements with him for provisions, I told him I was a sailor, and had left the king's ship in Acapulco; that I wanted to go and live up on the coast. . . . I told him we had money to pay him for all the favors he would do us; and, if he would bring us provisions . . . I would pay him his own price: but that he must act like a man, and not tell any one. . . . He said he was a poor man, but we might rely on him. . . .

We started with him, and, after going about half a mile through thick brush and vines, he told us to stop there — that he was going to bring us [a] gourd full of cocoanut-beer. In a short time he returned, bringing the beer. I gave him some money, and he returned to his cabin; and, in about two hours, he came with provisions, and we took breakfast. His wife also came with him, and brought some oil and rags to put on my feet; . . . [which] were very painful, [but] the thought of being free made me the happiest man in the world.

We stayed here three days, during which time the ranchero and his wife supplied us with fruits and provisions of all kinds. By this time my feet got so I thought I could continue my journey. My idea was, . . . when we got some fifty or sixty miles farther along the coast, I would buy a jackass, . . . to pack our provisions. Thus, in six months, I could reach the United States. When the good man brought us some fruit that evening, we told him we wished to start that night, and [to] bring us some provisions for the journey, and pilot us to the town of Atoaca. He said he thought I had better wait till my feet were cured, as the distance was about fifty miles. As I told him I thought I could travel, he went home and returned just at dark with provisions, and we set out. My friend the soldier had a sword: I had only a stick; for, having lost the cock off my gun, I had given it to the Indian ranchero.

We then took the road to Acoacan, through which we had to pass to go to Atoaca. When we came near enough to hear the dogs barking . . . , I told the pilot it was best to stop there, and for him to go on to the town, and, if he met any guard . . . he could tell them his wife was sick and he was going after medicine. The soldier said that was all right, but, as the barking showed the town to be distant, we could all go together some [piece] nearer. The pilot agreed with him; so we went on . . . three hundred yards farther, when we suddenly saw ourselves surrounded by about seventy men, who rose up on both sides of us! They demanded of us to surrender. The poor pilot sat down, and was taken. I spoke to the soldier and said, "Stand . . . close by me, and don't leave me, and we will escape." So we both charged — he with his sword, and I with my stick. As they had only swords and pikes, and no guns, we broke their ranks and went through together, and gained the thick woods.

After we had gone about half a mile . . . we came to a lake, about three hundred yards wide; and, notwithstanding such places are full of alligators, I plunged in, and the soldier followed. We waded a good distance, then swam a little, and then waded out to the flags and rushes. After hard work in getting through them, we got on dry ground, but in a great thicket of vines and thorns. We began to work through them as well as we could, without knowing what distance we were from any town or settlement.

Being fatigued, we stopped, and began to dry our clothes. My shoes were full of sand, and the skin not yet having grown on my feet, they gave me great pain. . . . It was just daybreak as we swam the lake, so we spent that day in the thicket. We cut down a cabbage-tree, and got the top out of it, which was all we had to eat.

The next morning we set out early, and worked through the forest till about sunset, when we heard a cock crowing at no great distance from us. We went in that direction, and came in sight of a small village, as we thought, though it was only the houses of some stock-keepers. I saw a pen that had some calves in it. I told the soldier we would retire . . . into the woods, and at night come back and kill a calf. . . . We had eaten nothing that day but some fruit. We returned to the pen [that] night, but the calves were gone. So we passed that place . . . and went on to see if we could find a road leading in the direction we wished to go. We soon got into a path that seemed to lead in the right direction, and we followed it till daybreak.

. . . We met a man, and asked him the distance to the next house on the road. He said the next place was the town of Caca-lutla, which was close by. We then concluded that our best way would be to conceal ourselves until night, and then pass by that village. We did so. The man we met was a constable, and returned back after we left the road, and raised two or three small villages. He had been informed of our escape the night before, and had orders to take us.

We went into the bushes, and lay down and rested till evening, without having eaten anything; and, before night, we set out on our journey. We went through some old farms, and passed around the town of Cacalutla, and fell into a road which led in the direction we wished to travel. About ten o'clock at night, we came to a small creek. We crossed it, and, just as we rose on the other bank, some thirty men sprang up and ordered us to surrender. We both stuck together, as we had done before — I with my stick, and the soldier with his sword. But in the first charge, a person behind the soldier struck him with a cutlass and disabled his arm, so that he could not fight. He then ran. Some of them pursued him; the others surrounded me. My feet were so sore I could not run, so I was forced to fight. I broke through them by knocking one of them down with my stick. But I did not get more than forty yards, when I was surrounded again. I was determined to be killed before [being taken]; but one of them . . . hit me . . . with a large stick, which knocked me senseless. When I came to myself, I was strongly tied, and saw my companion [beside] me in the same condition.

We were carried back to the village, where a new guard took charge of us and carried us back to Cojucan. Here we found our poor friend the ranchero, who had brought us provisions in the woods. Here I was ironed and put in the stocks, and two soldiers [were] left to guard us. . . . I spent that night without closing my eyes. The next morning . . . horses were brought, and we were carried again to Acapulco. I was taken to the governor, who, as soon as he saw me, said: "Oh, Mr. Bean, you have tried again to escape, but we deceived you; and I will put it out of your power to try it the third time. . . ."

He ordered them to take me back to the castle . . . [There he] . . . ordered them to bring a large mulatto, and had me chained to him. We were put in a room where there were some twenty prisoners. That night one of [them] whispered to me, that the governor had told the mulatto, if he would take care of me, he would deduct a year of his time; . . . I thanked him for the information.

This mulatto was very sulky, and said nothing to me. I was dubious . . . [because of] his great size, . . . but I was determined to try him the first word he said to me. Three days after I had been chained to him, we were taken out into the yard . . . to eat breakfast. As I [reached for] my bread, he jerked the chain, and threw me down. Near by . . . was half a bull's skull, with one horn on it. I [retreated] the length of my chain, got the skull, and struck him with it on the head, [knocking] him down. I continued my blows; he bellowed, "Murder!" the guard came and took the skull from me. . . . The news soon reached the governor, who ordered [the mulatto] to be separated and me to be flogged. But [I was not flogged]. I had a wheel put on my neck, so large that I could not reach the rim of it. Of all the modes of punishment, this was new to me. I could not move with it. I was in this situation four hours, when it was taken off, and I was taken back to my little cell with two pairs of irons on me.

Here I spent my time better. All was silent, and [there was] nothing to disturb me. I looked for my poor lizard, but he did not make his appearance. Two days [later], he came down the wall; but he had got wild, and would not come to me. At last I caught him, and he became as gentle as usual.

After Bean's latest attempt to escape, the last fraction of Spanish trust in him vanished — but only temporarily. The Viceroy himself ordered that Bean be sent to Manila, in "the first ship that sailed for that place." Instead of being depressed, however, Bean was pleased, still contemplating the possibility of somehow gaining his freedom in that faraway land and hiding among the savages he knew inhabited the region.

While he was awaiting a ship, there came to him an even more alluring possibility, one that grew largely out of two developments: French domination of the Spanish homeland that put a Napoleon on the throne there and alienated many Spaniards in the New World, and a long-smoldering hatred of the Spaniards and a yearning for freedom from their tyranny by the Mexican masses, who had been almost smothered by the military, the aristocratic landowners, and the church.

Three hundred miles to the north of Acapulco, in the mountain village of Dolores, an obscure parish priest named Miguel Hidalgo y Costilla loosed a conflagration that had been threatening for some time among the growing numbers of dissatisfied Creoles — Spaniards who were considered to have lost quality by having been born in Mexico — and mestizos — individuals whose ancestry was part Spanish and part Indian. Both groups were considered inferior to the pure-bloods born in Spain, as were — certainly — the masses of Indians, who occupied the lowest level. Now many of these people of "inferior" birth became determined to drive out or to exterminate the European-born Spaniards, and Hidalgo ignited the revolt on September 16, 1810, with the *Grito de Dolores* — Cry of Dolores. The rebellion unleashed passions so extreme in their cruelty that many of the dissident Creoles were driven from an initial sympathy with the revolution to support of the government, after all. Later, when Hidalgo and a fellow conspirator were seized and executed in 1811, another priest, malaria-plagued José María Morelos y Pavón, would assume leadership of the revolutionary forces.

A threat to Acapulco by this same Morelos in November of 1810 gave Bean his own chance for independence from Spain. The tattered rebel army that advanced on the seaport was much more imposing in numbers, some three thousand men, than in arms, which included bows and arrows and other primitive equipment. Nevertheless, the concern of the Spanish officers at Acapulco grew to such an extreme that they offered to free prisoners who promised to fight for the King. Bean, ironically, thus gained his freedom: he volunteered to serve the sovereign who had held him prisoner for nearly a decade, and his captors released him from the wretched cell, freed him from his irons, and armed him with a gun and a sword. For fifteen days he drilled with royal troops, without having any intention of fighting on their side. He was waiting quietly for the arrival near Acapulco of the revolutionists, to whom he intended to desert.

His chance came one morning when he and other troops were embarked aboard a vessel sent to look for Morelos' forces, known to be nearby. After a short cruise they were put ashore near the mouth of a stream. There the Spanish commander asked for volunteers to scout for the revolutionists, and Bean quickly offered himself. Seven others joined him.

They followed the stream inland for about three miles, then the others halted momentarily. Bean said he would go on ahead "and look out for the enemy."

. . . I soon saw a company of the patriot militia. I stepped to one side of the road, and they did not see me till they came up. They had done duty at the fort, and knew me. I spoke to them. They said they knew I would not fight against them, and were overjoyed to see me. I told them there were . . . below [seven soldiers] . . . that they could go and take them. They did so, and not one escaped . . . .

We were immediately taken to the camp of Morelos, where he had about one hundred and fifty men, and about twenty old broken guns. They told him who we were, and he said he wanted us to assist him in the struggle. I, for one, told him I was a republican, and that was what I had come for.

So, after ten years, Bean again had a country. He was to devote himself faithfully to revolutionary aims until, finally, Mexico had her independence. During that time he would serve as Morelos' aide and chief powder-maker, would fight well in Morelos' first important victory at Tres Palos, would marry a Mexican woman — Magdalena Falfan de los Godos — of legendary beauty and devotion, would "almost forget his own language," it was said, in his absence from the United States.

When Bean finally returned to his native land in 1814, almost four years after his release from prison, it was to be as an agent for the Mexican revolutionists seeking — unsuccessfully — to organize an invasion of Spanish Texas. By chance he would arrive at New Orleans just before Andrew Jackson defeated the British there, and Bean, a quick volunteer, was to fight ably with a group of artillerymen furnished by a newly made friend, Jean Laffite.

It seemed entirely appropriate that Bean should fight at the Battle of New Orleans in the company of men whose long-time allegiance was in great doubt. He belonged with them: because he happened to ride out with Philip Nolan that autumn day in 1800, he was destined to live out his life with torn loyalties.

15. THE GENERAL ON TRIAL

THE SITUATIONS of Bean and Wilkinson — when compared in 1811, shortly after Bean had joined Morelos — described an extreme irony of fate, at least temporarily. Bean, far from his native land, had found acceptance among Mexican revolutionaries, after ten years of enforced banishment from virtually all connections. Wilkinson, a high officer of the army in his own United States, was, on the other hand, again meeting vigorous rebuffs from his fellow citizens.

Important people still sniped at him, Congress continued to talk investigations, and Daniel Clark, Jr., published *Proofs of the Corruption of General James Wilkinson and of His Connexion with Aaron Burr*, which convinced many more people that Wilkinson had had alliances with both Spain and Burr, although it was not legally conclusive.

Again, Wilkinson's staunchest supporter seemed to be his wife. In March of 1810 he had married a sophisticated young woman of Louisiana, Celestine Laveau Trudeau — "my divine little Creole" — to whom he gave the same devotion he had once reserved for Ann, and who returned the dedication in equal measure, despite their striking difference in ages: he was fifty-two, she, just past twenty.

The continuing talk of Wilkinson's political and military impropriety now began to embarrass the Madison administration, which had succeeded Jefferson's, and again the President called for an investigation, this time in the form of a court-martial, at Fredericktown, Maryland. It convened in the summer of 1811.

Wilkinson faced charges of being an accomplice of Burr's and once more of being paid for services to Spain — and of various derelictions arising from his misadministration of an army post at Terre aux Boeufs, in fetid Louisiana swampland that was infested with flies and mosquitoes. At this unfortunate location, chosen by Wilkinson himself, the unhealthful surroundings, bad rations, and shamefully inadequate hospital facilities had resulted in the deaths of half of the two thousand troops assigned to duty there, despite their eventual removal to a more wholesome location near Natchez.

Again Wilkinson insisted he had devoted himself to his job in a manner that had been, as usual, exemplary. The poor administration and the deaths had not really been his fault, but were due to the inefficiencies of other persons, he claimed. Concerning his exposure of Burr's plot he said, "I was not content . . . with the bare discharge of my duty. I did more.

— To save from disgrace, the man, who had so long been my friend, and to save my country from the dangers and disasters, his irregular and enterprising spirit, might bring upon it; I sought to give his distinguished talents, a proper object of ambition."

Less complimentary to Wilkinson's conduct were three witnesses who testified against him — men with whom he had once been friendly, but who later turned on him, as people were inclined to do. Wilkinson spewed his invective at all three, without regard to ethics, taste, or — probably — the truth. One of them, the New Orleans businessman Daniel Clark, Jr., Wilkinson labeled as treacherous; another, the Spanish agent Thomas Power, he described as being without principle.

For his onetime friend Andrew Ellicott, the surveyor, he reserved his most violent abuse. He depicted Ellicott as an immoral man — the implication being, of course, that his testimony against Wilkinson was worthless.

The General's attorneys introduced a deposition, ridiculous in its vilification of Ellicott — and even of Ellicott's son — that apparently was considered seriously by the court. It contained declarations supplied by one of Ellicott's former assistants, a man who had a record of drunkenness and of being absent without leave while in Ellicott's employ. His statements were in the form of answers to questions asked by Wilkinson himself about the surveyor's adulterous relationship, during the time he was engaged in the boundary survey, with a maid who accompanied the party.

The General, who had employed the man after Ellicott dismissed him, elicited this statement from the deponent:

". . . It was said, and generally believed, that [the] extraordinary trio, father, son, and washerwoman, slept in the same bed, at the same time — I did not see, but I believed it. I was even pressed myself by the old sinner, Ellicott, to take part of his bed with his washerwoman and himself, for the night."

Wilkinson dug further into this. "Was it not your opinion, and that of all the other gentlemen of the party, that Ellicott, the father, and son, held criminal intercourse with the said harlot Betsy?"

"It was my opinion, and I understood it to be the opinion of every gentleman of both parties, American and Spanish, that the Ellicotts, both father and son, held, and continued a beastly, criminal, and disgraceful intercourse, with the said harlot Betsy."

Such was the tone of Wilkinson's defense. Small wonder that Daniel Clark, Jr., whose philanderings were common, had been reluctant to engage the General head-on during the court of inquiry earlier, choosing instead to work through John Randolph. Again Wilkinson was exonerated, but again the respite from his critics was brief.

A second court-martial, in 1815, stemmed from Wilkinson's performance in the war with England. One of his major assignments had been completed satisfactorily enough: the occupation of West Florida — an area in what is now eastern Louisiana, southern Mississippi, Alabama, and Florida — on orders of Congress. The United States had claimed the area as part of the Louisiana Purchase, but Spain had disputed this and continued to maintain a few troops there. Despite their presence, Anglo-American settlers moved into the country, and in 1810 proclaimed independence from Spain as a "Republic of West Florida" and asked for annexation to the United States. Three years later, when the United States was at war with Great Britain — which was simultaneously allied with Spain against Napoleon — Congress ordered Wilkinson to take his troops into West Florida and occupy it, ostensibly in response to annexation requests but also to prevent its use by the British as a base of operations. The Spaniards withdrew without fighting.

Wilkinson failed, however, in another assignment. Later he had been transferred to the northern frontier, and during an abysmal campaign against Montreal his defective leadership had resulted in a great defeat of the American forces, at a time when they appeared to be only three days away from the city.

Some persons claimed that the General had bungled even more than that. They said he had been drunk on at least one occasion during the campaign and had been guilty of other scandalous conduct.

All these accusations figured in the charges: neglect of duty, drunkenness, and conduct unbecoming to an officer. "If guilty," Wilkinson implored, "let my punishment be exemplary — if innocent, acquit me with honour. In the last event I shall not have lived in vain." He pleaded not guilty, of course, before the court, which was convened initially at Utica, New York.

Once more Wilkinson squirmed out from under the lid of justice. The appearance of drunkenness, he said, actually had been brought on by medicinal doses of laudanum; and the Montreal fiasco was not really his fault, but due to the inefficiency of others. Wilkinson's typically verbose alibis, offered to fellow officers from a small army, made the charges, which had been vaguely worded anyway, impossible to prove. Wilkinson again was "honourably acquitted of all . . . of the charges and specifications against him exhibited."

This time, however, exoneration did not save his army

career. During his court-martial the war with England had
ended, and Congress began at once to halt appropriations for
the army and to cut its size. A general of Wilkinson's stature
was no longer needed; nor were many other officers of higher
caliber and greater promise.

The future seemed clouded, even for Wilkinson. Where
might an old general approaching sixty find opportunity, when
most of it seemed behind him and never had been fully in
his grasp, even though he had reached out for it? His chances
had passed through his own slippery hands: his affinity for
double-dealing, his pretense, and his self-centeredness had
eventually barred the way to his own ambition by alienating
those who could have, and otherwise probably would have,
helped him to any of his many goals.

Wilkinson did not acknowledge these faults in himself, of
course, and possibly never even suspected them. If there ever
was a man who could rationalize, it was the General.

Now there was no young Kentucky, no empty expanse of
Mississippi River, not even the army to turn to, to recoup his
most recent loss in the manner to which he had become accustomed. Politics still attracted him, but no major office was
available for a man of Wilkinson's hue.

Jobs there were: in fact, President Madison offered him a
selection, in an effort to silence his embarrassing harangues
against the "persecutions" that continued to plague him,
even after the courts-martial, and against the government that
would be so dastardly as to drop a man who had served it so
long and so well. The General scoffed at all of the offers,
and determined, instead of condescending to accept any of
them, to write his memoirs. This would serve him in two
ways: he would make an immortal contribution to history,

and he would, finally and conclusively, expose and humiliate those who had questioned his honor. His father's parting advice would be followed in an entirely appropriate manner. Also, Wilkinson calculated, he would probably make a great deal of money from his literary production.

The complete *Memoirs*, published in 1816 in three volumes with an atlas, were a perfect reflection of Wilkinson. They were ostentatious, verbose, disorganized, full of talk of persecution, absolutely humorless, but still laughable in their depiction of the author's importance. Nevertheless, the work contained some valuable history of the Revolutionary War.

Before presenting these memoirs of his "own times," Wilkinson piously bowed himself "submissively before the Most High, without a murmur at his decrees." Then he remarked, "Should [these volumes] furnish a salutary lesson to my contemporaries or posterity — should my misfortunes or my errors prove useful, and the enmity which I have experienced serve as a beacon to other men, I shall feel perfectly recompensed."

Early in the first volume appeared an introspection, the first of many:

> Every man who enters into the trusts of a nation, owes to it an account of the manner in which he has performed his duty. A service of more than thirty years under innumerable vicissitudes, has been closed in a manner, which leaves it questionable with many, whether I have been the victim of my own misconduct, or of ministerial perfidy — of private intrigue, or gross and vindictive persecution; which last has been the too frequent fate of the most faithful and disinterested men in all ages, and under every form of government, although the reproach of such conduct has been particularly attributed to republics.

Looking upon myself, at the close of a long agency, as accountable to the great republican family of which I am a member, and aware how liable the actions and characters of men are to be discoloured by misrepresentation, these memoirs will serve to make the community better acquainted with the transactions in which I have been concerned, and the mode in which I discharged my public duty, than personal prejudice and powerful influence have hitherto permitted. . . .

My transgressions against the laws of my Creator have been too many, but they have been venial; and I trust I have found their remission in a contrite heart.

Wilkinson's book was dedicated "To The Citizens of The United States." For the title page he chose a fatalistic passage out of literature, one that must have seemed to him to personify his life.

> — *Remember that the ways of Heaven,*
> *Though dark, are just: that oft some guardian power,*
> *Attends unseen, to save the innocent!*
> *But if high Heaven decrees our fall — O let us*
> *Firmly await the stroke; prepared alike*
> *To live or die.*

Sales of the *Memoirs* eventually proved to be disappointing. In the first flurry they were substantial enough, encouraging the General to muse over the possibility of further writing, particularly more documentation of the Revolutionary War. When subsequent book receipts failed to pour in to match his high expectations, however, his interest flagged, and he turned to other fields.

He maintained his interest in business and politics, speaking out on many subjects as in the old days, and he bought a plantation in Louisiana. Finally, however, it was the country to the west that attracted him.

His age now was too far advanced to permit him seriously to consider plans about an empire there, if indeed he ever had any, but the independence movement in Mexico attracted his interest: perhaps he was unconsciously reverting to the glorious, untainted days of his youth and of the American Revolution, when virtually all of his associates had acknowledged his talent, ability, and promise.

In March of 1822 he left Louisiana for Mexico City, where he hoped he might one day be appointed United States minister. After his arrival there, he wrote President James Monroe to suggest this, but received no reply. No matter: because of his background and experience he would be sought as an adviser by Mexican officials, he was certain, and he would collect money owed by the Mexicans to a Baltimore firm for weapons furnished during the revolution against Spain. For this work he was to receive a 15-percent commission. Finally, he would create a general aura of good will by presenting to the Mexican Congress a Gilbert Stuart portrait of Washington, a man whom the recently freed Mexicans admired.

Wilkinson succeeded, as of old, in ingratiating himself with the highest authorities, including the Mexican dictator Agustín de Iturbide, former royalist, for whom he prepared a memorial containing his wisest suggestions for beneficial relations with the United States. He maintained these cordial relations with subsequent officials during the frequent government changes. Again he was disappointed financially, however, and times once more become difficult for him.

To his sons Joseph and James he wrote plaintive, pitiful letters asking for assistance. "If your Father has ever done aught to serve you," he wrote Joseph in 1825, "he now implores you to reciprocate and to save his credit, his feelings, his Character

and His Liberty. . . . Oh my Son! I conjure you not to fail me
— let me hear from you as soon as possible, and favourably,
on this subject, and it will be the means of restoring my Health
[and] of prolonging my Life. . . . Oh how sweet it is to me to
find that your trust is in God, in whose mercy I put my whole
trust and confidence, amidst all my troubles, whence-so-ever
they may oppress me, and who indeed, whatever may have
been the afflictions put upon me, has never abandoned me, in
any extremity, praised be His Holy Name." About the same
time he wrote James to say he had drawn one thousand dollars on him: ". . . and I must conjure you not only to be ready
to accept [the bills] but punctually to honor them, as my
reputation is at hazard."

The possibility of being awarded an empresario grant occupied him in the spring of 1825. Approval would mean that he
would be given coveted land holdings for dispensing, as he
saw fit, to settlers in Texas. He failed in his quest, however,
possibly because he was incapable, despite his general popularity in Mexico, of inspiring genuine trust.

Wilkinson also failed to collect the debt from the Mexican
government, and eventually he tried to settle for fifteen thousand dollars. Discouraged, he yearned to return to his home
in Louisiana, to his "divine Creole" Celeste, and to the son
and daughter she had given him; but his work was not finished.

Toward the end of 1825 his health failed rapidly; his intake
of laudanum and opium, to relieve various pains, grew to a
high level. Celeste came to him from Louisiana, and was at
his side when he died, three days after Christmas.

General James Wilkinson was buried in a cemetery in Mexico City. Although many notables attended his funeral, he
soon lay forgotten, and later his body was exhumed and

placed, along with all others in the cemetery, in a common burial chamber. Thereafter no one could be certain of the exact location of the General's place of interment, except that it was in a country that was not his.

Still, he lay quietly and tranquilly, in contrast to the turmoil of his life. In his *Memoirs* he had remarked, "I have suffered many and grievous persecutions, alike unprovoked and unmerited, which were frequently produced by the most meritorious acts of my life." In his ponderous style he denied ever wronging a fellow man or omitting any occasion within his circumscribed sphere to discharge his duty to his neighbor and to his country with zeal and fidelity.

To his credit, none of the charges against him had been proved, and he died with his name legally clear, even if some people still spoke of him in a derogatory manner.

The ordeal had ended for him now. People would surely acknowledge their great debt to him and let him rest peacefully.

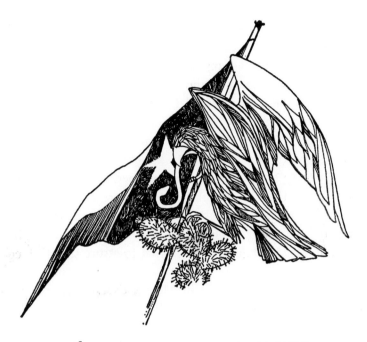

16. A DIVISION OF LOYALTIES

IN THE DECADE following General Wilkinson's death Peter Ellis Bean, a man approaching his fifties, was about to be swept into the whirlpool of another revolution, this one in Texas. There, in the early 1830's, increasing dissatisfaction among Anglo-American colonists would soon erupt in war against Mexico.

The trouble stemmed less from differences in race, religion, and language than from friction generated by Mexican politics. The central seat of government, Mexico City, lay almost a thousand miles away, overland across a wilderness of desert and mountains that held many dangers poised to strike at travelers entering that forbidding region. Even the state capi-

tal was far distant — in Saltillo, where it had been located in
1824, when the Mexican government combined the states of
Texas and Coahuila because of scarcity of population in Texas.
Being removed so far from supreme authority resulted in some
advantages, but it also caused frustration. The instability of
the Mexican government, which was wracked by frequent
revolutions after independence from Spain finally had been
gained in 1821, added further to the confusion.

Even more grating to the Anglo-Americans, however, was
the effect of the Mexican alarm at the increasing numbers of
settlers in Texas, and the attempt to shut off the flow. Mexico
tampered with the economic situation, too: slavery was abol-
ished, and customhouses were erected to assure the strict collection of taxes.

Had government officials in Mexico City been more con-
siderate and knowledgeable of Texas problems, rebellion
might not have broken out, at least not when it did. Antonio
López de Santa Anna, who became president in 1833, could
easily have placated the Texans. They at first supported him,
in fact, believing him to be a man of liberality who would
work in their behalf. Instead, he garrisoned a strong military
establishment throughout the combined state of Texas and
Coahuila — mostly in Texas — and antagonized the colonists
even further. At Gonzales, seventy miles east of San Antonio,
the first serious fighting of the Texas Revolution occurred in
October of 1835, when Mexican troops sought unsuccessfully
to take a cannon from a group of embittered Texans.

By a fortune that seemed to have evolved inevitably from
his tragically twisted life, Bean, an Anglo-American, entered
these troubled times as a colonel of Mexican cavalry commanding the "Eastern Department" — Texas — where he
also served as Indian agent. The early Texas historian Hen-

derson King Yoakum said of this circumstance, "In the contest which seemed to be now approaching, neither party appeared willing to trust him."

The background was this:

Bean's loyalties were fully divided, even to the extent that he had wives in both Mexico and Texas: Magdalena Falfan de los Godos in tropical Jalapa, near the Gulf coastal city of Veracruz, and Candace Midkiff, a lively, teen-age Tennessee girl with whom he had formed a "matrimonial alliance" during a visit to his native state in 1818. While his wife in Jalapa waited, wondering if her husband were still alive, Bean resided in the United States with Candace for five years before moving back to Mexican territory — with Candace and a son, Isaac — to a place near Nacogdoches, the town where he had been held a prisoner by the Spaniards nearly a quarter of a century earlier.

He had been able to reach Tennessee, and his second wedding, through the very selflessness of his Mexican wife, if a story told by one of his descendants is not too much exaggerated. The account appeared in editions of the Dallas *Morning News* and the Galveston *Daily News* of November 24, 1901.

Bean had returned to Mexico after his first visit to the United States — during which he fought the British at the Battle of New Orleans — in February of 1815, bringing arms he had been able to buy, although he had not been successful in stirring up an invasion of Spanish Texas. Then in mid-1816, following a decisive defeat of Morelos by royalist troops, Bean had concluded that his cause in Mexico was hopeless and that the Spaniards would surely execute him if they caught him.

With his recent bride Magdalena he fled eastward, on

horseback, along the Mexican coast, hoping somehow to find a ship that would carry them both across the royalist-controlled Gulf of Mexico to safety in the United States. Spanish cavalry pursued them, however, and in the chase, "Bean's horse had . . . about given out and [Bean] was well aware that capture meant death. His faithful wife suggested that he mount her horse and escape. . . . There was no time for parley, and dismounting in sight of the pursuing cavalry, the exchange was quickly made. As Bean embraced his wife in parting she thrust a silk handkerchief and a black mantilla into his hand. Mounting the horse recently ridden by his wife, Bean fled."

His wife is said to have been captured by the Spaniards, released, and returned to her home in Jalapa. Bean made his way to the United States, probably on a ship, and on to Tennessee, where he entranced Candace with exciting stories of his adventures in a faraway land — no doubt eliminating reference to Magdalena — and won her in the same manner that Philip Nolan had won Frances Lintot two decades earlier. Perhaps coincidentally, Candace's father was said to be rather well off financially.

With Spain still in control of Mexico, Bean dared not return to his once-adopted homeland, but in 1823 — when he and Candace moved to their new location near Nacogdoches — Mexico had finally been given its independence, and the Spaniards were gone.

Bean and his wife and child settled on a fertile red-land prairie some thirty miles west of Nacogdoches, near three Indian mounds. Mound Prairie was, in fact, the name of the site. During his previous five years of toil Bean had enjoyed success as a farmer, and Candace apparently had inherited something upon her father's death; so they came to Texas with money and an impressive number of personal possessions.

Soon after their arrival a daughter was born. Within two years, however, Bean had departed this domesticity to go to Mexico, where old friends of his from revolutionary days headed the Mexican government. Upon his arrival they greeted him joyfully as a long-absent brother, commissioned him colonel in the army, and received his application for empresario. Coincidentally, at the same time James Wilkinson sought the same concession, and the two men perhaps met.

Bean's application proved to be detrimental to him, for in it he made note of his marriage to Magdalena Falfan de los Godos, with whom he no doubt lived during his visit to Mexico. When it became known to the officials that Bean had another wife on his farm near Nacogdoches, considerable consternation ensued, and they commenced an investigation of him.

From Saltillo the governor of the state of Texas and Coahuila, in a letter dated October 20, 1826, ordered his deputy administrator in Texas to have a "trusty and honest" person observe Bean: to ascertain his conduct toward his wife Candace, to learn whether he supported her and the family and lived "maritally" with her, and to determine if she acknowledged him as her lawful husband.

Apparently no one was actually assigned to observe Bean, but several persons who claimed to know him well were later questioned, and their replies varied, perhaps according to their personal feelings about him.

One man responded that Bean had been in company "with

very bad people"; another said he was "an honest man" although "he is very fond of boasting and telling large stories about his exploits in the Mexican revolution." A colonist who was much respected recalled traveling on one occasion from Memphis to Columbia, Tennessee, with Bean, who said then he was going "to the neighborhood of the place where he married his wife." Still another man declared he had known Candace's father and did not believe he was a man who would have permitted his daughter to live with a man to whom she was not legally married.

Candace herself appeared before an alcalde in 1826 and declared she had indeed been married to Bean by a Mr. McDaniel in Tennessee. Later, in a move to clear himself with the Mexican authorities in regard to the double marriage, Bean forced Candace to sign a statement certifying "she never was" married to him, and that she had said so previously only to save his property in event of his death.

Nevertheless, evidence supported the fact that he had been legally married to Candace, but this bit of propriety did not help him at all with the Mexican authorities. Because of his dual marital status they decided against appointing him empresario, although he retained his commission as colonel.

Bean's dilemma, already great, actually increased, at least in regard to Candace. While he was away from his Texas home and in Mexico for a nineteen-month period, she married another man, thinking, as she said, that Bean was dead. He returned three days after the wedding, and the bridegroom — warned in advance of Bean's impending arrival — moved out of the connubial nest. With what emotion Bean greeted Candace after hearing of this can only be imagined: some neighbors told later of his beating her after he returned, and

Mexican authorities later were to record: "Coming to his house, Col. Don Pedro Elias Bean mistreated his wife with sticks and blows and chased her out of his house." Some people said the Beans did not live together after that, but there is evidence to the contrary.

Whatever happened, Bean was not a man to be very understanding of Candace's bad judgment, which he likely considered treason. Later they did indeed separate, and Candace married again. Her new husband abandoned her, however, and she and Bean lived together even after that.

With himself, Bean was considerably more indulgent than with Candace. Years later, an early-day Texan who claimed to know the facts declared that Bean, while holding a commission as colonel in the Mexican cavalry, made many official trips to Mexico City, and while there lived with his "senior wife" — Magdalena. This same man said that after it had become commonly suspected that Bean had two wives, Bean admitted to his Texas neighbors that he did indeed have a woman in Mexico, but not a wife, only a mistress; and to knowledgeable Mexicans he claimed that the Texas woman was not a wife, but a mistress.

Slipperiness had become his outstanding trait. By evading involvement in a Nacogdoches battle, in 1832, between supporters of two Mexican factions, he worked himself into promotion as commandant of the garrison. When followers of the supposedly liberal Santa Anna rose against the government of Anastasio Bustamante, the appointed Nacogdoches commandant dutifully summoned his troops and opposed the rebels in the name of the entrenched government — and was defeated. Colonel Bean happened to be taken ill about this time, but the historian Henderson King Yoakum remarked of his indisposition, "Bean, not wishing to lose his commission, did not take part in the contest."

Bean proved to be even more fortunate than he expected. Santa Anna deposed Bustamante, and the defeated Nacogdoches commandant, having supported a loser, shared Bustamante's fate. The new government, searching for a satisfactory commandant for the garrison, chose the untainted Bean.

Equally clouded were Bean's true feelings during the Texas revolution, when he held the Mexican army commission as colonel, yet lived amicably with his Anglo-American neighbors. Even today, historians study his inconsistent record and speculate on his honest sympathies. Probably they were such that he would have been with the winner, no matter which side it happened to be.

When revolution approached, Bean obviously opposed it. In the latter 1820's, in fact, he had helped to quell an uprising of Anglo-Americans termed the "Fredonian Rebellion" — following a dispute about land titles. At that time he had written the rebel leader, "A rupture with the Mexican Nation, to whom I have the honor to belong, must prove fatal to you."

Bean had been highly effective in persuading the Indians not to join the Fredonians in a dangerous alliance that possibly would lose Texas for Mexico; he triumphantly reported in a letter obviously of his own composition that he "maid Pease" with the Indians. To a leading chief, Richard Fields, who leaned toward rebellion, Bean wrote a most cordial letter during negotiations assuring him of the "good will and intent" of Mexico. Fields was not placated by words, however, and Bean was forced to try another maneuver. He recounted it in a dressed-up letter of February 7, 1827, to the military commander of Texas:

I have the satisfaction to report to Your Lordship that on the 25th ult. I received the visit of the Cherokee, Tabano, Delaware, and Kikapoo chiefs who had been engaged in the rebellion, and I induced them to embrace the party of the Republic of Mexico. I succeeded in pursuading them that they had been deceived by Fields. They killed him. . . .

After killing the chief as a "traitor and rebel," the Indians called to the attention of the Mexican government the sad fact that Fields left a widow and seven small children, all unable to support themselves — they possessed only a few cattle, but numerous debts — and they petitioned the government to act as father to the children, a gesture of which Bean no doubt approved.

The Fredonian Rebellion drew the opposition of most Anglo-Americans in Texas, and Bean's part in quelling it did not necessarily indicate his opposition to them. On the eve of the Texas revolution, however, he still seemed to be at times a staunch supporter of the Mexican government. In a letter written August 18, 1835, he informed the military commander at San Antonio that other men "trying to spread rebellion" were attempting to form an alliance with the Indians, but he doubted their success "because the Indians are not disposed to be hostile to the Mexicans." Nevertheless, he suggested sending troops to the frontier "in large numbers, to impose respect; otherwise the stationment . . . of a small party of soldiers would induce the disaffected to persevere in their mischievous designs." He asked permission to visit San Antonio to report in person about "other business of importance," because he suspected persons, presumably pro-revolutionaries, of opening his mail at San Felipe. At other times, however, Bean had seemed to try to disengage himself from such involvement. He concentrated instead on acquiring real estate, and he built up extensive holdings.

During the war he asked to be taken into custody as a Mexican officer: thus he could later claim his pay from Mexico while in an arrest status, yet avoid the regular duties, which might have been not only embarrassing but unpleasant. After the war, however, Bean swore as a Texas citizen, in an application to the Republic of Texas for a league and a labor of land: "that I was a resident citizen of Texas at the date of the declaration of Independence, that I did not leave the country during the Spring of 1836 to avoid a participation in the struggle, that I did not refuse to participate in the war, and that I did not aid or assist the Enemy, that I have not received a title for the quantum of Land to which I am justly entitled under the Constitution and Laws. . . ."

Long after the revolution ended, long after Bean had died, debate was to continue as to his true sympathy during the war. Evidence pointed toward the Texan cause — certainly Bean's relations with its followers were cordial — but the fact was that neither Texans nor Mexicans could trust him implicitly, as the historian Yoakum had observed, because of his attachments to the other side. His most effective work around this time happened to benefit both factions: maintaining peace among the Indians.

"[Bean's] acceptance of a parole from an officer of Texas, as a Mexican prisoner, and his purpose to require Mexico to pay for his services, indicated he was not in sympathy with the Texas Revolution," a Texan of historical prominence later remarked. "His living in Texas so long during and after the Revolution, in amity with the people, and his obtaining a headright for land as a citizen of Texas, would tend to a different conclusion."

Bean did not even have a consistent name, as Bennett Lay has noted in *The Lives of Ellis P. Bean,* the only full-length biography, in English, of that perplexing man. Bean signed his name Ellis P., P. E., Peter Ellis, Pedro E., and even Ellis H. The Mexican revolutionists knew him as Pedro or Elias, or both. Lay used Ellis P., because, he pointed out, Bean usually signed his name that way for the first forty-three years of his life. Bean's son Isaac, however, had become familiar with another signature, and he once corrected a writer: "I see you have goten my Fathers name wrong you have it Ellis P. Bean when it should of bin P. E. Bean. . . ."

Bean's splintered life was the more tragic because it was not necessarily of his own choosing, but evolved accidentally from his joining Philip Nolan's last expedition. Although he was a resourceful, resilient, energetic, self-contained individual, genuine happiness eluded him, judging by his wanderings: when he was in the United States he yearned for Mexico; when he was in Mexico he longed for his native land. With his loyalties divided, none of them could be firm.

Finally he seemed to make a choice. The attraction of his beloved Magdalena was great, and he knew she yearned for him. A story told by the New Orleans newspaperman George Wilkins Kendall indicated the extent of her desire.

Kendall had been captured in 1841 along with other members of an armed "Texan Santa Fé Expedition" sent by the new republic of Texas with the intention of adding part of New Mexico to its domain. The captives were held for many months in Mexico before being sent to Veracruz for sea transportation home. At Jalapa they stopped at a *hacienda.* Kendall described the visit:

> We entered the dwelling, the front of which was almost concealed from view by creeping vines and different species of

rose and other flowering bushes. The mistress of this sylvan
retreat, a stout, handsome-faced woman . . . instantly beset
us with inquiries in relation to some American she had known
formerly — a colonel she called him, but the name I do not
remember."

The "handsome-faced woman" surely must have been Magdalena. Now Bean would go to her. In February 1843 he
wrote out his will at Nacogdoches. "Owing to the great oncer-
tainty of this mortal life . . ." he began, as his reason for draw-
ing up the document at that time. The statement seemed to
be his own biography in brief, especially appropriate with his
misspelling of "uncertainty." In it he left all of his property
to his three children — two sons and a daughter — "I own
and acknowledge." By this time he and Candace were no
longer man and wife.

Then Bean rode out of Nacogdoches for the last time —
to New Orleans, where he boarded a ship for Veracruz, in the
country where he had been held against his will for such a
long time. At Jalapa, in the *hacienda* of his "senior wife," he
passed his last years, crippled with rheumatism, yet torn by
old longings. "When the weather becomes cool," he wrote
a Texas friend in 1844, "[you] will see me."

His health never permitted another trip. On an autumn
day in 1846 he died, forty-five years after the death of Philip
Nolan, and twenty-one years after General James Wilkinson.
In Bean's other home, Nacogdoches, the property he had
accumulated and willed to his children was largely frittered
away in lawsuits.

17. RETRIBUTION

TWO HUNDRED MILES west of the Mexican town of Jalapa rested the body of another expatriate. James Wilkinson, lying under the soil of Mexico City, would have been pleased by certain developments in the West, had he known of them. Probably he would have been given an important military command in a coming campaign, especially with his knowledge, however acquired, of the country involved.

The United States finally had begun moving with force in the direction that had attracted Wilkinson's lifelong ambitions. In 1845 the Republic of Texas effected its annexation to the United States, which was not content to stop at the western boundary of the new state, wherever that was.

The boundary was, in fact, a bone of contention that eventually led to United States expansion to the Pacific. Mexico, which had self-consciously — and with false pride — warned that the annexation of Texas would lead to war, declared that the western limit of that territory, which Mexico had never recognized as a republic, was delineated by the course of the Nueces River, a hundred miles or so east of the Río Grande. If this was true, it meant elimination of a large section of what is now Southwest Texas: from the present Brownsville to Corpus Christi, and an expansive slice to the northwest.

Texas, however, claimed the Río Grande as its western boundary. The United States naturally accepted this contention, and sent an army to that river, where a battle soon raged with Mexican troops. President James Polk claimed that the Mexicans had fired first, and the United States declared war in May of 1846.

Whether Polk spoke with sincerity has been debated by many historians. In his diary he recorded one aim of his administration as being the acquisition of California from Mexico. Presumably he would have been willing to take the territory in peaceful purchase had Mexico been willing to sell, but a war certainly would enable him to get it. In the end he got not only California — giving Mexico a fifteen-million-dollar consolation for its loss — but also New Mexico and Texas to the Río Grande.

Wilkinson would have approved of all this. Despite his frequent inconsistencies he had been unswerving in his belief that his own, and the nation's, future lay to the west.

For Wilkinson, the future had, of course, too soon become the past, and now, even in death, the past was not to let him rest.

For all his betrayal of friends, his love of money easily acquired, and his pomposity, pretense, and self-importance, the one flaw in his character widely spoken of but never proved had been his treachery. "I have not said I held no private correspondence with the governors of Natchez and New Orleans," he wrote in his *Memoirs*, concerning the days of Spanish rule, "but I do deny that such correspondence was . . . injurious to my country or dishonorable to myself."

Unfortunately for Wilkinson's niche in history, the rumors of his remunerative work in behalf of Spain found corroboration, long after his death. What Daniel Clark, Jr., had written of during Wilkinson's lifetime — but had not proved conclusively — in *Proofs of the Corruption of General James Wilkinson and of His Connexion with Aaron Burr*, and what many people had suspected, was, in fact, true. Wilkinson had indeed been paid by the Spaniards, not only as a civilian but also while he had been the ranking general of the United States Army.

The evidence was uncovered later in Spanish archives, some of it found in collections taken in Havana after the Spanish-American War, some dug out of documents in the voluminous holdings in Seville and in Madrid and Mexico City. In the Madrid archives an American researcher, William R. Shepherd, found a copy, in Spanish, of an oath of allegiance to Spain that Wilkinson had written out in 1787, when he had sought trading privileges on the Mississippi River.

Shepherd reproduced an English translation of his discovery in an article, "Wilkinson and the Beginnings of the Spanish Conspiracy," in the April 1904 issue of *The American Historical Review*. Although this was not a translation of the original oath, of course, but of its Spanish version, the wording, as Shepherd remarked, was without any doubt Wilkinson's.

The oath was, as usual, verbose and pompous, and it was filled with rationalizations that only a self-seeker like Wilkinson would have had the stomach to accept. "Self-interest regulates the passions of nations as well as of individuals," he began, "and he who imputes a different motive to human conduct either deceives himself or endeavors to deceive others."

Wilkinson made a point, but this represented quite a change of attitude for a man who had claimed, loudly, to have received "a sense of justice" and "Christian faith" from his mother. He thought hard on the subject — or pretended to, in the oath — before finally indulging his own self-interest: "When a person of distinction intends to expatriate himself," he wrote, "he ought to proceed with extreme caution and circumspection."

Wilkinson implied that he did just that, pondering "the obligations which subsist between him and his country." He mulled them over, and decided he could consider himself free to switch his loyalty with as little ceremony as a common-law marriage:

> Having these principles, and holding to this opinion, I hope that no one can say of me with justice that I break any law of nature or of nations, of conscience or of honor, in transferring my allegiance, from the United States to his Catholic Majesty.
>
> Born and educated in America, I embraced her cause in the recent revolution, and steadfastly I adhered to her interests until she triumphed over her enemy. This event, having rendered my services no longer needful, released me from my engagements, dissolved all the obligations, even those of nature, and left me at liberty, after having fought for her welfare, to seek my own.

Wilkinson then declared he had determined to seek his welfare through the offices of Spain, without wishing his native country ill, and that he felt sure his conduct would be "directed by such principles of loyalty to my [adopted] sovereign, and of justice to my fellow subjects as will assure me tranquillity of conscience and bear my name untarnished to posterity."

He pledged his service to the "interest and aggrandizement" of the King of Spain, and signed this oath on August 22, 1787. The fact that he later requested his first payments from commercial transactions to be deposited for him in the Spanish city of New Orleans indicated he meant to play this game of intrigue honestly with the Spaniards, although some of Wilkinson's defenders have claimed otherwise.

Many more documents were uncovered, in Madrid and elsewhere. Correspondence between Wilkinson and the Spanish governor of New Orleans, Esteban Miró, beginning immediately after Wilkinson's first visit to New Orleans, discussed, in a cipher early agreed upon, mutual plans for commercial enterprise and even for empire. Also discussed was a "memorial" written out by Wilkinson, in return for New Orleans trading privileges, in which Wilkinson suggested the best course for Spain to follow in her competition with the United States on the North American continent. Included in these files, too, was a copy of Wilkinson's proposal before a Kentucky Assembly in which he urged a complete break with the United States, as had been rumored at the time.

Lengthy letters, translated from code, from Wilkinson to Miró and, later, to Carondelet and Gayoso, the succeeding governors at New Orleans, offered further advice on American politics; destroyed the reputations of certain fellow citizens who from time to time attempted to get commercial privileges from the Spaniards, as Wilkinson had done; recommended twenty-two notable Kentuckians for Spanish pensions upon their agreement to work for separation of their territory from the United States and for its subsequent acquisition by Spain; suggested raising a volunteer force of a thousand Kentuckians for defense of Spanish Louisiana during a threat of war between Spain and England in 1790; advised a strengthening of Spanish fortifications against attack by the United States, but added that as long as he, Wilkinson, commanded the United States Army Spain need not worry; pleaded for anonymity — "for the love of God" — and warned that the suspicions of Washington, the man, and of Congress were "wide awake," and that spies had been detailed to observe his activities.

Wilkinson wrote these letters as both civilian merchant and ranking general of the United States Army: his acceptance of a military commission obviously had not deterred him from his intrigues. An annual pension of two thousand dollars had, in fact, been awarded him by Spain after his return to American military service, according to a letter from Carondelet dated February 1, 1792. This "retainer" the Spaniards made retroactive to January 1, 1789. Another letter showed that two years later Wilkinson had asked to have the pension increased to four thousand dollars.

Records of the money given Wilkinson proved conclusively that it had been in payment for his service as a Spanish agent in the United States. By the close of 1796 he had received a total of thirty-two thousand dollars for this work, and even more was to come in later.

Some documents illustrated Wilkinson's remarkable propensity for double-dealing. Although he sought commercial privileges on the Mississippi River for himself and certain associates, he urged that Kentuckians at large not be allowed access to the river. Only by keeping it closed, Wilkinson said, could Spain hope to separate the Western Country from the United States and persuade it to accept Spanish domination — by allowing its tradesmen use of the river.

The archives showed that soon after his first visit to New Orleans Wilkinson began a practice of writing letters of introduction to Governor Miró for fellow Kentuckians to carry with them when they traveled down the river to settle or to engage in commerce. The archives also revealed, however, that Wilkinson had an understanding with Miró that unless the Governor received a second letter from him, separately sent, in behalf of any particular individual he was not to consider seriously the first recommendation.

Another exchange of correspondence showed that while Andrew Ellicott, the surveyor, had been venting his anger on the Spaniards for their slowness in evacuating posts along the Mississippi, Wilkinson, the general, had been in calm, even cordial, correspondence with Carondelet regarding the matter. Documents also recorded the fact that the Spaniards had delayed evacuating their posts along the Mississippi with the hope that the Western Country could still be enticed away from the United States, and river navigation thus be reserved for Spain.

Wilkinson apparently even used his suggestions to the individual nations in a complemental manner. He would, for instance, advise Spain to strengthen her fortifications along the border, then quietly excite United States interest in the country across that same border, so that Spain, sensing the pressure stemming from his anonymous prick, would value his advice even more highly and presumably, then, would pay him better for it.

Another letter attested to the treachery not only of Wilkinson, but also of Philip Nolan, and it repudiated conclusively a piece of evidence that Wilkinson had introduced in his behalf in the 1808 court of inquiry, in an attempt to show that money received from Spain had been for early tobacco shipments, not for service as a Spanish agent, as alleged.

Before that court Wilkinson had produced the statement in Nolan's handwriting, accounting in detail for certain money received from New Orleans as having come from commercial transactions, and the court had declared that the correctness of the document was "highly probable," but that it did not really matter: ". . . if [General Wilkinson] did receive the money, as stated, the transaction was fully justifiable, and if he did not receive it, there is no proof of his having received it at all."

Now, in the Spanish archives, a letter from Wilkinson to Carondelet — written in 1796, during Wilkinson's military days — told the truth about the matter. In it Wilkinson declared that if he should be questioned about his receipt of Spanish dollars he would say they had come to him, belatedly, as a result of his earlier commercial activities. "To circumstantiate this assertion," he added, "I will cause the faithful Philip Nolan . . . to make an account in form with a letter of advice dated at New Orleans last autumn. . . ."

At least one incriminating letter even turned up in the French archives. After Louisiana had been returned by Spain to France, and shortly before its purchase by the United States, a noted New Orleans citizen wrote the Paris govern-

ment, "The Spanish government . . . was assisted by a powerful inhabitant of Kentucky . . . who will put the same zeal at
the command of France." The writer added that the "powerful" Kentuckian first visited New Orleans in 1787, which
could only have been Wilkinson. The General also corre-
sponded occasionally with British agents and seemed to be
as willing to negotiate with them as with anyone else.

The Spanish files particularly gave up many letters from
Wilkinson pleading for more, more money and for greater
secrecy to cover his intrigues. Once Wilkinson asked to be
referred to only as "No. 13," and never by name, in all correspondence. He became No. 13 indeed, and a lucky one at
that, since none of this material had been available to any
of the investigators during his lifetime.

Instead, his word had been widely accepted: for example,
that the idea of "alienating" Kentucky from the jurisdiction
of the United States, as he had written in his *Memoirs,* was so
ridiculous that no man of character or good will "would have
ventured to hazard it."

Still other incriminating documents were found by the historian I. J. Cox in the archives at Seville and described by him
in an article in the July 1914 issue of *The American Historical
Review:* "General Wilkinson and His Later Intrigues with the
Spaniards." These records included a letter from the Spanish
governor of West Florida, Vicente Folch, with whom Wilkinson had worked, for a fee of twelve thousand dollars, to preserve that coveted territory for Spain. This was before
Wilkinson himself led troops into the area, on the orders of
Congress, and occupied it for the United States during the
War of 1812.

Folch's letter proved to be ironic in its accuracy.

My dear friend: I believe that you are already well convinced that I have acted as is befitting a faithful servant of
the noble Spanish Monarchy, and that I have sincerely ful-
filled the obligations which friendship imposes upon me. I
have done even more, for I have sent to the archives of Havana
all that pertains to the ancient History [meaning Wilkinson's
intrigues with the Spaniards], persuaded that before the
United States are in a situation to conquer that capital you
and I, Jefferson, Madison, with all the Secretaries of the different departments, and even the prophet Daniel himself will
have made many days' journey into the other world.

On the other hand, Wilkinson seemed just as ready to betray
Spain as the United States, and he obviously did this, too.
The Spaniards never retaliated by exposing Wilkinson's
treachery, as they could have done easily and perhaps were
tempted to do, because they would have besmirched their
own national name by exposing the intrigues.

Wilkinson was adept also at working the two countries
against each other, and he tried whenever possible to bring
a third party, like Great Britain, into the juggling. For all his
treachery, however, he was a comic-sad character: as an agent,
he hurt no one very much, although he might have had intentions of doing so. Nor was he especially helpful to anyone,
except for his early military service during the American Revolution and, later, for his work in helping to open up the Mississippi River to western trade — a result stemming indirectly
from his own selfish efforts to get from the Spaniards special
consideration, which he required in any venture to come near
success.

Disregarding the legal and moral implications of betraying
one's own country, his greatest offense probably was against
the Spaniards, of whom he made fools over a long period of

time by taking their money and giving them little, actually, in return; but he gave no one very much in return.

Wilkinson's ultimate ineffectuality could be attributed to paucity of purpose and absence of integrity. His only true concern was for his personal welfare, a trait that can only shrivel a man's capacity and his soul. Had he given his native land his devotion, his considerable abilities might have earned him a place of stature in its history, although he never would have stood on the same level as Washington, Jefferson, or Franklin. Had he worked faithfully for Spain, he could have been an infinitely more effective and a more dangerous agent in the United States. The documents found in the Spanish archives, considered in historical context, showed that he did neither.

Of all his many faults, however, Wilkinson's greatest shortcoming was that he never realized — or at least never acknowledged — any of them. The General died convinced of his own worth: how else could a man not only endure the countless attacks he had faced but return them with such pure venom? The archival discoveries conclusively exposed his true character, but at a time so late that only history was able to render a just verdict on him.

Nevertheless, his absolute refusal to take an inventory of himself, and his continued scheming, lost him the trust of many fellow men, and surely contributed to "the worst solitude," which Francis Bacon defined, "to be bereft of sincere friendship."

18. AN EPILOGUE

THE THREE MEN without countries — Wilkinson, Nolan, and Bean — certainly were not all villainous. Each man showed courage and other fine qualities on countless occasions, and each displayed a few obvious loyalties besides self-interest: Wilkinson to his wife, Nolan to Wilkinson, and Bean to the Mexican revolutionists. Furthermore, despite their shiftiness, all three were typical in many ways of the westerners of that day.

Men who desired the benefits of more firmly established government remained in the eastern states, as did those individuals who preferred to adhere to Old World mores. These were people who chose conventionality in exchange for the security and comfort of a known way of life. Allegiance could be expected from them.

The West, however, was new, and its white settlers encountered many new problems: the absolute necessity of access to the Mississippi River for commerce was only one of them. In the eighteenth century no one ventured across the Appalachian Mountains unless he had tired of what might be called the "establishment" of those days or unless he sought new opportunity. Frontiersmen were by nature unconventional and independent, intrepid and sometimes foolhardy; and they were often supremely self-seeking. The westward movement gave to American society its emphasis on competition and its general willingness to forgive almost anything for the attainment of "success."

The Frenchman Alexis de Tocqueville saw this tendency soon after its appearance, and voiced his tolerance of it — in its habitat. The restlessness, independence, and ambition pushing Americans westward to new opportunity contributed to the unequaled prosperity and well-being of the United States, he said; but he added that these same forces in Europe would have been an extreme threat to Old World society. "Such is the present good fortune of the New World," Tocqueville wrote, "that the vices of its inhabitants are scarcely less favorable to society than their virtues."

The Spaniards saw this tendency, too, but they were much less tolerant of it, since their properties stood in the path of the human deluge.

José Vidal, the Spanish commandant at Concordia, across the river from Natchez, often voiced his distrust of Americans — perhaps with good reason, considering his failure to stop

Nolan's unauthorized last expedition by legal means. On October 4, 1803, he wrote the governor of Texas.

> The United States have purchased Louisiana from France; and if they succeed in establishing themselves on the limits of Texas, God keep us from their hands. I appreciate, dear sir, that you do not know the Americans, and particularly their government, which is the most ambitious, restless, unsteady, caviling and meddlesome government on earth. I am so disgusted with them that I long for the moment of parting with them after fourteen years' residence on their borders.
>
> There may be good men and they are the most industrious people in existence, but of what avail are the good elements when the government lacks the force to keep down the rabble which predominates in that country? I know from experience that rigor is the only means to restrain it between bounds. . . .
>
> The Americans have generally eminently insinuating manners; they are educated, but conceal under their hypocrisy the venom in their hearts. They study the Spanish genius, usages and manners, and shape their plans after that knowledge. They master their passions, capitulate with their conscience, dissemble their politics; the Protestant passes himself off for a zealous Catholic, and the spy for a faithful subject of the Spanish Government.

Other Spaniards echoed Vidal, ignoring the history of their own nation's conquest in the New World. A general headquartered in San Antonio remarked, "Self-interest and lure [are] the only object of the Anglo-Americans, who care not whence it comes." Pedro de Nava, whose troops had sought out the intruder Philip Nolan, said, "These people care little about exterior worship, and are ever ready to convert to their own advantage all that which is more sacred in our religion."

These same Spaniards, by their reactionary methods in restraining trade, closing borders, and trying, ostrichlike, to wish away the Anglo-American presence, only hastened their own demise on the North American continent. The Americans had not been restrained by natural boundaries like the Appalachian Mountains; neither would they be bound at this momentous time by artificial political lines, especially since these borders could be defended only poorly. Exclusion merely served to arouse curiosity and to make the forbidden territory seem more attractive, as the activities of Wilkinson, Nolan, Bean, and many other men, showed.

Some questions present themselves to a casual reader of late eighteenth- and early nineteenth-century American history. A few of them are still unanswerable.

What was actually happening in the western United States and in the nearby Spanish possessions? Was some sort of new empire, independent of either nation, near reality? Were Spaniards, as well as Americans like Wilkinson, really involved in such an intrigue, as the surveyor Ellicott had indicated in his letter when he wrote: "The apparent zeal of the Spanish officers on the Mississippi for the dignity of the crown, is only intended to cover their designs till the great plan which is the establishment of a new empire is brought to maturity. Their principles are highly revolutionary."

A 1797 letter from the Spanish governor at New Orleans, Carondelet, to his agent Thomas Power would seem to corroborate Ellicott.

You will examine with care; and you will endeavor to discover with your natural penetration, the General's [Wilkinson's] dispositions. I doubt that a person of his character would prefer, through vanity, the advantage of commanding the army of the Atlantic States, to that of being the founder, the liberator, in fine, the Washington, of the Western States;

his part is as brilliant as it is easy; all eyes are drawn towards him; he possesses the confidence of his fellow citizens, and of the Kentucky volunteers; at the slightest movement, the people will name him the General of the new republic; his reputation will raise an army for him, and Spain, as well as France, will furnish him the means of paying it. On [his] taking Fort Massac, we will send him instantly arms and artillery, and Spain limiting herself to the possession of the forts of Natchez and Walnut Hills, as far as fort Confederation, will cede to the Western States, all the Eastern bank to the Ohio, which will form a very extensive and powerful republic. . . .

This letter is suspect, however, because Wilkinson quoted it in his *Memoirs*, obviously to intimate that a western republic with which gossip had linked him was not his idea. Nevertheless, the letter — written when Carondelet had sought to delay evacuation of Spanish posts along the Mississippi with the hope of splitting off the Western Country from the United States — could well have been genuine in its content. Although one would suppose Carondelet knew Wilkinson's "dispositions" thoroughly through the General's secret letters to him, Wilkinson's character certainly was slippery enough to persuade Carondelet to carry out some verification on his own.

Serious involvement of high officials of New Spain in any Anglo-American plot to carve out an empire from Spanish lands was unlikely, although some of them were indeed allied with Wilkinson and probably Nolan, and other Americans, in confidential money-making enterprises. Spanish archives would not have bared the extent of this, as they did Wilkinson's treachery to the United States, because the officials involved would never have allowed the retention of incriminating documents.

In New Orleans, and elsewhere in Spanish Louisiana, a

more logical time for highly placed Spaniards to have supported the carving out of an empire in Spanish territory would
have been the period 1808 to 1813, when Napoleon, after invading Spain, installed a Bonaparte on the Spanish throne.
This event led to disaffection in Mexico and contributed to
the revolutionary outbreak there. By 1808, however, the
United States possessed Louisiana, and the Spaniards had
departed.

Neither was the founding of a permanent empire in the
Western Country of the United States ever really close to
actuality after Kentucky became a state in 1792 and Tennessee
in 1796, and especially after the free navigation of the Mississippi River had been assured some time later, following a
series of disputes with Spain over the matter.

Wilkinson's betrayal of Burr showed what the chances were
for any successful western move, whether in United States or
Spanish territory. The General would not have helped to
bring Burr to trial had he smelled the sweet possibility of
attainment.

Another question looms out of this period: how was Wilkinson able to evade justice when it is now known, and was
even then suspected, that he was a traitor to the United States
throughout much of his career? Several answers become
obvious, in addition to the one foremost: that Wilkinson
wangled the support of Jefferson and other influential persons
at critical junctures in his life.

Another reason was the coarseness of his time and place,
which rendered difficult a refined delineation of anybody or
anything. It was widely rumored, for instance, that Wilkinson's correspondence with the Spaniards and with important
Kentuckians — supposedly concerning commercial transac-

tions — was carried on in cipher. In that unsophisticated day, however, encoded letters were not unusual. Many people wrote them that way, because the primitive carriers liked to open mail and read it for amusement during their long, lonesome journeys, and because eventual delivery at the destination intended was precarious.

Probably the most important reason for Wilkinson's success in avoiding an appropriate justice, however, was a lack of communication throughout the country. Rumors usually remained rumors; gossip was only gossip. In this day of mass media the General would not have been able to hide from television, radio, and newspaper coverage: some reporter would win a Pulitzer Prize for exposing him. In his day, however, he not only remained behind a curtain, but he sometimes used talk of his intrigues to get what he wanted — such as promotion.

Alexander Hamilton once wrote George Washington to urge promotion for Wilkinson, although he added, "I am aware that some doubts have been entertained of him, and that his character, on certain sides, gives room for doubt." He favored promotion, he said, because Wilkinson, if passed over, might in disgust really become what people only suspected of him. Washington agreed: "It would feed his ambition, soothe his vanity, and, by arresting discontent, produce the good effect you contemplate."

Usually Wilkinson somehow got at least a portion of what he wanted — except genuine happiness — and his life's purpose was clear: complete dedication to his own welfare. The intent of his protégé Nolan was not so obvious, however, and this raises another question: what was Nolan's aim, especially during his puzzling last expedition into the Spanish domain?

No doubt Nolan's immediate goal was to accumulate wealth — something he never did. Corralling those hundreds, even thousands, of wild horses was work much too strenuous for him to have used it merely as a cover for other activity. Nevertheless, numerous documents in both English and Spanish attest to his exploration and mapping of little-known lands. The knowledge and information he accumulated, however, was never used in any conquest — and, oddly, no map known to have been prepared by Nolan can be found today.

Numerous conflicting accounts regarding his last expedition continued to be recorded after his death. His second-in-command, David Fero, declared to the Spaniards who captured him that Nolan had said he intended to take from Texas two hundred and fifty mustangs to sell in Kentucky and pay off debts — but Fero would not have told the Spaniards if Nolan's actual intentions had been more ominous than that. On the other hand, the deserter from Nolan's expedition, Mordecai Richards, asserted — in addition to his statement quoted earlier in this book — that Nolan possessed maps and "explored everything more attentively than a man would do who had not other ends in view than that of catching horses"; but Richards was, of course, probably telling the Spaniards what he knew they expected to hear.

Andrew Ellicott's relationship with Nolan increases the mystery surrounding Nolan's purpose. Ellicott knew Nolan's patron, Wilkinson, for what he was — a Spanish agent — but he never voiced any suspicion that Nolan was in this category, too. Obviously, then, Nolan convinced Ellicott of his genuineness, although the documents from Spanish archives have since shown that Nolan knew very well what Wilkinson was up to. Nolan lied to Ellicott about Wilkinson's good intentions, and he continued to work faithfully with the General in all his intrigues. Once he wrote Wilkinson, "What do you think of Ellicott? he professes great friendship for me."

Possibly Nolan informed on Ellicott to the Spaniards during and after his trip with Ellicott down the Mississippi to Natchez for the boundary survey. Nolan obtained his passport to Texas soon afterward, and he would have used almost any means of ingratiation to help get it.

Ellicott's letter to the Department of State about Wilkinson and the western plot also stirs speculation about Nolan. "Genl Wilkinson is to proceed from Kentucky with a body of troops . . . into New Mexico [meaning Texas] . . . — the route has been already explored." If the route truly had been explored for Wilkinson, only Nolan could have done it at that time, because this was before Wilkinson dispatched the expeditions of Pike and others.

If Nolan was mapping Spanish lands for conquest, he was doing it, no doubt, for Wilkinson and not for Thomas Jefferson or anyone else. Such exploration by Nolan seems logical — likely, in fact — although it was never put to use. A conclusion as to the reason for his last expedition, however, is more difficult to make. Without reinforcements of strongly armed Anglo-Americans he could not have hoped to conquer the Spanish domain — not, at least, without Indian help. Yet the possibility of reinforcement never became evident, and Nolan did not attempt to enlist the Indians. Despite all this, Nolan seems deliberately to have aroused the hostility of the Spaniards both before and during his last expedition, and he surely anticipated an attack by them. He was a swaggering man, as shown by his boasts before his last departure that he could defeat any force the Spaniards could muster; but did he really believe he could succeed against such odds?

One man of intelligence and education seemed to think Nolan might have been foolhardy enough to believe this. William Dunbar of Natchez wrote in a letter after Nolan's death:

> I am much concerned for the loss of this man. Altho' his eccentricities were many and great, yet he was not destitute of romantic principles of honor united to the highest personal courage, with energy of mind not sufficiently cultivated by education, but which under the guidance of a little more prudence might have conducted him to enterprises of the first magnitude.

"Every man is the maker of his own fortune," said Sir Richard Steele, and the three men in this book bear him out in ways already described. Steele might have added that every man is the maker also of history, in a way however slight, and these three again would have borne him out.

History would not have been noticeably different, however, had Wilkinson, Nolan, and Bean never been born. Wilkinson was a general; but he was no Washington — nor a Benedict Arnold — in ability. Nolan, it is claimed, fired the first shots in the United States conquest of the western section of the continent, and a historical marker near the site of the battle asserts — with false directness — "Nolan's death aroused a wave of indignation that led to the independence of Texas"; but if Nolan had not been there another American would have filled the role later. Bean, with his knowledge of powder-making, proved to be invaluable to the rebel Morelos, but even without Bean Mexico still would have had her independence at the same time she was given it.

The importance of these three lies in the fact that they were typical of men of their times. They certainly were not "heroes" — not even Nolan — although they might have been, and often were, courageous. Each man was selfish but occasionally selfless; strong, but frequently weak; intelligent, but sometimes bumbling; capable, but often overconfident. Each seemed to have more than his share of human power and, at the same time, more than his share of weakness. All three were men of action, and as such they left a larger mark on history than most men do. Furthermore, whether they realized it, and whether Americans care to admit it, all three helped to carry the flag to what has been called its Manifest Destiny.

Primarily, however, all three were tragic characters, and they were tragic because they were, for whatever reason, actually without a country. Although they "carried the flag," they did it unintentionally and certainly haphazardly: their involvement was almost wholly with themselves.

BIBLIOGRAPHY

BIBLIOGRAPHY

Most of the material on James Wilkinson came from the sources listed below. My account of Wilkinson is not meant to be complete, of course, but to discuss his activities only as they pertain to Philip Nolan or to the tone of this book. For those who want the whole story of Wilkinson, the best biography is *Tarnished Warrior*, by Major James R. Jacobs.

Cox, I. J. "General Wilkinson and His Later Intrigues with the Spaniards," *American Historical Review*, July 1914.
Green, Thomas Marshall. *The Spanish Conspiracy: A Review of Early Spanish Movements in the South-West.* Cincinnati: Robert Clarke, 1891.
Hay, Thomas Robson, and M. R. Werner. *The Admirable Trumpeter: A Biography of General James Wilkinson.* Garden City, New York: Doubleday, Doran, 1941.
Jacobs, Major James R. *Tarnished Warrior: The Story of Major-General James Wilkinson.* New York: Macmillan, 1938.
James Wilkinson Letters. The University of Texas Archives.
Langford, Nathaniel Pitt. "The Louisiana Purchase and Preceding Intrigues for Dismemberment of the Union," *Collections* of the Minnesota Historical Society, Vol. IX. Saint Paul: The Society, April 1901.
Mathews, Catharine Van Cortlandt. *Andrew Ellicott: His Life and Letters.* New York: Grafton, 1908.
Shepherd, William R. "Wilkinson and the Beginnings of the Spanish Conspiracy," *American Historical Review*, April 1904.
Shreve, Royal Ornan. *The Finished Scoundrel.* Indianapolis: Bobbs-Merrill, 1933.
Wilkinson, General James. *Memoirs of My Own Times.* 3 vols. with atlas. Philadelphia: Abraham Small, 1816.

Most of the material on Philip Nolan came from The University of Texas Archives Collection, specifically from the Bexar Archives, Mirabeau B. Lamar Papers, Miscellaneous Documents Relating to Philip

Nolan, Nacogdoches Archives, Philip Nolan Documents (photostats of a large original collection in the Yale University Library), and the Robert Bruce Blake Papers (translations of part of the Nacogdoches Archives.) In some cases the originals of these documents are in the Texas State Library. Quotations from translated letters have been used as those translations appear in the archives. Other material came from the sources listed below.

No full-scale biography of Philip Nolan exists. The most thorough writing on his life to date has been "Philip Nolan and His Activities in Texas," a thesis, by Maurine T. Wilson, that was never published.

Carter, Hodding, with Betty W. Carter. *Doomed Road of Empire: The Spanish Trail of Conquest.* New York: McGraw-Hill, 1963. (Also contains material on Wilkinson.)

"Concerning Philip Nolan," Texas State Historical Association *Quarterly,* April 1904.

Cox, I. J. "The Louisiana-Texas Frontier," Texas State Historical Association *Quarterly,* July 1906.

Ellicott, Andrew. *The Journal of Andrew Ellicott.* Facsimile (originally published 1803). Chicago: Quandrangle Books, 1962.

Hale, Edward Everett. *The Man Without a Country.* (Originally published in *The Atlantic Monthly,* December 1863.) First edition in book form, with an introduction by Van Wyck Brooks. New York: Franklin Watts, 1960.

Hale, Edward: *Philip Nolan's Friends: A Story of the Change of Western Empire.* New York: Scribner, Armstrong, 1877.

Hale, Edward Everett. "The Real Philip Nolan." *Publications of the Mississippi Historical Society,* Vol. IV, ed., Franklin L. Riley. Oxford, Mississippi: The Society, 1901.

Hill, Robert T. "The Present Condition of Knowledge of the Geology of Texas." U.S. Geological Survey Bulletin, No. 45. Washington, D.C., 1887.

Hunter, Theresa M. "Romance Sketches from Early Texas History," Dallas *Morning News,* November 18, 1928.

Loomis, Noel M. and Abraham P. Nasatir. *Pedro Vial and the Roads to Santa Fe.* Norman: University of Oklahoma Press, 1967.

Murry, Elizabeth Dunbar. *"Early Romances of Historic Natchez."* Natchez: Natchez Printing and Stationery Co., 1938.

"Phillip Nolan: 'The Man Without a Country,' " New Orleans *Daily Picayune,* May 15, 1864.

Quintero, J. A. "Philip Nolan and His Companions," *Texas Almanac,* September 1868 (Galveston, W. Richardson).

Wilson, Maurine T. "Philip Nolan and His Activities in Texas." Unpublished Master's thesis. The University of Texas, Austin, June 1932.

Most of the material on Peter Ellis Bean came from Bean's lengthy *Memoir* in Yoakum's *History of Texas*, listed below, and from The University of Texas Archives Collection, specifically from the Bexar Archives, Nacogdoches Archives, Peter Ellis Bean Papers, and the Robert Bruce Blake Papers.

An excellent biography of Bean can be found in *The Lives of Ellis P. Bean* by Bennett Lay. As was the case with Wilkinson, I have not attempted to tell Bean's complete story, only as much as is pertinent to Nolan and to the tone of this book.

Fuller, H. C. "Ellis P. Bean," Dallas *Morning News*, November 24, 1901.
Lay, Bennett. *The Lives of Ellis P. Bean*. Austin: University of Texas Press, 1960.
Yoakum, Henderson King. *History of Texas from Its First Settlement in 1685 to Its Annexation to the United States in 1846.* Facsimile (originally published 1855). Austin, Texas: Steck, 1935.

The following articles and books were used for background material. In some cases their early dates of publication rather than quality of writing made them of interest.

Abernethy, Thomas Perkins. *Three Virginia Frontiers*. Gloucester, Massachusetts: Peter Smith, 1962.
Allen, William B. *A History of Kentucky*. Louisville: Bradley and Gilbert, 1872.
Anthony, Irvin. *Paddle Wheels and Pistols*. New York: Grosset & Dunlap, 1929.
The Audubon Nature Encyclopedia. 12 vols. Philadelphia: Curtis Publishing, 1965.
Baldwin, Leland, D. *The Keelboat Age on Western Waters*. Pittsburgh: University Press, 1941.
Bancroft, Hubert Howe. *History of the North Mexican States and Texas.* 2 vols. San Francisco: History, 1889.
Brackenridge, Henry Marie. *Views of Louisiana: Together with a Journal of a Voyage up the Missouri River, in 1811.* Facsimile (originally published 1814). Chicago: Quadrangle Books, 1962.

Claiborne, J. F. H. *Mississippi, as a Province, Territory and State, with Biographical Notices of Eminent Citizens.* Jackson, Mississippi: Power & Barksdale, 1880.

Crocket, George Louis. *Two Centuries in East Texas: A History of San Augustine County and Surrounding Territory from 1685 to the Present Time.* Facsimile (originally published 1932). Dallas: Southwest Press, 1962.

Davidson, Marshall B. *Life in America.* 2 vols. Boston: Houghton Mifflin, 1952.

Dobie, J. Frank. *The Mustangs.* Boston: Little, Brown, 1952.

Encyclopedia Americana. 30 vols. New York: Americana Corporation, 1954.

Hall, James. *Sketches of History, Life and Manners in the West.* 2 vols. Philadelphia: Harris and Hall, 1832.

Henderson, Archibald. *The Conquest of the Old Southwest.* New York: Century, 1920.

Kendall, George Wilkins. *Narrative of the Texan Santa Fé Expedition.* (Originally published 1844.) Chicago: Lakeside Press, 1929.

King, Grace, and John R. Ficklen. *Stories from Louisiana History.* New Orleans: L. Graham, 1905.

Newcomb, W. W., Jr. *The Indians of Texas: From Prehistoric to Modern Times.* Austin: University of Texas Press, 1961.

Quaife, Milton (ed.). *The Southwestern Expedition of Zebulon M. Pike.* Chicago: Lakeside Press, 1925.

Rightor, Henry (ed.). *Standard History of New Orleans, Louisiana.* Chicago: Lewis, 1900.

Texas Almanac and State Industrial Guide, 1968–1969. Dallas: A. H. Belo, 1967.

Webb, Walter Prescott, and H. Bailey Carroll (eds.). *The Handbook of Texas.* Austin: Texas State Historical Association, 1952.

Weems, John Edward. "A Gateway to a Gaining Nation: Nacogdoches, Texas," *A Vanishing America: The Life and Times of the Small Town.* New York: Holt, 1964.